Serpents in the Classroom

Serpents in the Classroom

THE POISONING OF MODERN EDUCATION
AND HOW THE CHURCH CAN CURE IT

BY THOMAS KORCOK

Serpents in the Classroom: The Poisoning of Modern Education and How the Church Can Cure It

© 2022 New Reformation Publications

All rights reserved. No part of this publication may be reproduced, distributed, or transmitted in any form or by any means, including photocopying, recording, or other electronic or mechanical methods, without the prior written permission of the publisher, except in the case of brief quotations embodied in critical reviews and certain other noncommercial uses permitted by copyright law. For permission requests, write to the publisher at the address below.

Unless otherwise indicated, all Scripture quotations are from The ESV® Bible (The Holy Bible, English Standard Version®), copyright © 2001 by Crossway, a publishing ministry of Good News Publishers. Used by permission. All rights reserved.

Published by:
1517 Publishing
PO Box 54032
Irvine, CA 92619-4032

Publisher's Cataloging-In-Publication Data
(Prepared by The Donohue Group, Inc.)

Names: Korcok, Thomas, author.
Title: Serpents in the classroom : the poisoning of modern education and how the Church can cure it / by Thomas Korcok.
Description: Irvine, CA : an imprint of 1517 Publishing, [2022] | Includes bibliographical references and index.
Identifiers: ISBN 9781948969741 (hardcover) | ISBN 9781948969758 (paperback) | ISBN 9781948969765 (ebook)
Subjects: LCSH: Education (Christian theology) | Education—Religious aspects—Christianity. | Education—Philosophy. | Christian education.
Classification: LCC BT738.17 .K67 2022 (print) | LCC BT738.17 (ebook) | DDC 261.5—dc23

Printed in the United States of America

Cover art by Brenton Clarke Little

To Milo, Lydia, and Bonnie
So we can play together in the eternal garden

Contents

Introduction xi

Part I Bitten by the Snake xv

How Theology Shapes Pedagogy 1
    The Twentieth Century Educationalists:
    A Case of Snakes in Sheep's Clothing 4
    The Enlightenment 5
    The Secular Humanists and Marxists 8
    The Gnostics 19
    Conclusion 28

The Venom of Liberal Education 29
    The Uncritical Thought of Critical Thinking 30
    Gnosticism and Education 34

Striking Where It Hurts 41
    The Rejection of Truth Through Revelation 43
    The Rejection of Original Sin 48
    The Rejection of Authorities Instituted By God 51
    The Rejection of Christian Catechesis 57

The Effects 63
    Harm to Individuals 63

> Harm to the Church 65
> Harm to Society 67

Part II Applying the Antidote 69

The Cure Of Timeless Standards 71
> The First Standard: Goodness 72
> The Second Standard: Beauty 73
> The Third Standard: Truth 76
> The Standard That Binds It All Together: Unity 77
> Using the Standards the Wrong Way 79

Treatment Protocols 87
> Content and Methods 87
> The Curriculum of the Christian School 90

A Classical Liberal Arts Education:
The Training of Christian Thinkers 105

Conclusion 111

Appendices 115
> Appendix 1: Comparison of Classical Christian Education
> and Liberal Education 115
> Appendix 2: J. C. Vonderau's Learn-by-Heart
> Schedule for Hymns 118
> Appendix 3: Matching Hymns for the Six Chief Parts
> of Luther's Small Catechism and the Augsburg Confession 120

Notes 123

Bibliography 139

Scripture index 145

Subject index 147

"The person in whom Christ's life is not, in him the true Good, and the Truth have never been known."
—Frankforter, *Theologia Germanica*

Introduction

"That's just your opinion" was the retort of a pert 13-year-old girl as I explained the scriptural perspective of "same sex marriage." It came in the middle of a talk to a class of 13 and 14-year-olds in which I made the daring claim that society's new definition of marriage was contrary to the law of God. To this girl, it did not matter that I had spent years studying theology, or had devoted careful thought to this issue, or could cite clear scriptural proof for what I was teaching. This child, who barely knew the words of the 6th Commandment, had no compunctions in telling me that God's holy and ancient Law was, in fact, subject to personal opinion. To her mind, what I was teaching was not sound doctrine, but my own views, and her views were equally valid.

This wasn't the first time I had come across that mindset—and it certainly wouldn't be the last—but it did make me wonder about what enabled her to think in this way. What made it possible for this girl to elevate her personal opinion above the revealed Word and reject the clear teaching of Scripture? A generation earlier, that way of thinking was completely foreign, especially within the church. But for this girl, like most of her peers, it was now the default position.

Years later, I had moved from being a parish pastor to a university professor and was teaching a course on Christian education to student teachers. We were meeting in a College of Education classroom, and on the walls were charts highlighting major educational thinkers of the twentieth century—people like John Dewey, Maria Montessori, and Jean Piaget. During one session, I realized that I was short of lecture material, and therefore announced a group work assignment. The students were to research what those educationalists taught, believed, and confessed.

The results were eye-opening. As a college student, I had learned about these educational thinkers, and like my students, I was led to believe that they were all unbiased researchers whose theories were theologically neutral which could (and should) be incorporated into Christian education without any concerns. My impromptu class assignment revealed something quite different, however. We discovered that all of them had very strong theological views and saw education as a means of advancing these views. A further study of these and other influential educators made clear to me why the young girl in my class, years earlier, so readily rejected the Word of God. Her schooling—not only what she had been taught, but how she had been taught to think—had shaped her mind to reject orthodox Christian theology and accept the alien theologies of these educationalists.

The educational establishment has gone to extraordinary lengths to make it appear that these theories are based on solid, scientific, unbiased research. The underlying theological agenda is not readily seen. However, peeling back the rhetoric, one quickly sees how these foreign theologies have shaped everything from teaching methods to curriculum choices. In both secular and Christian colleges of education, student teachers are taught not to address children as "boys and girls" but as "friends." The use of red pens for marking assignments is discouraged. Games of elimination are banned. Teachers are to be learning guides instead of subject matter experts. Content-based education is discouraged. Learning outcomes stress individual fulfillment. Teaching methods are built around the dogma of individual learning styles. While advocates will claim that these are all "research-based"—a claim designed to shield them from criticism—they are all, to one degree or another, expressions of the theological beliefs of influential educationalists. Few teachers (and, I suspect, professors of education) are theologically literate enough to recognize these beliefs. This poses a danger for the Christian educator who, ignorant of the theological underpinnings of these teaching methods, cannot rightly judge their ability to properly form and nurture young Christian minds.

One expects to find philosophies contrary to the Christian confession in secular schools; but how do they find root within schools of the church? The reliance on state licensure for teachers, the acceptance of government funding of college programs, the desire to attract more students, and the general lack of Christian research have created an environment in which Christian colleges of education have uncritically incorporated many of these theories and methods with little thought toward their theological ramifications.

Not only has the church unwittingly opened the door for these alien theologies, but she has also abandoned her own rich educational heritage. Though rarely acknowledged, the truth is that the church lays claim to some of the greatest educational thinkers of all time, who over centuries developed an approach to education that promoted sound theology and developed right-thinking Christians. To grasp how closely theology and education are related, one has only to look at the multitude of theological giants who wrote knowledgably and passionately about education. Augustine of Hippo, Rabanus Maurus, Thomas Aquinas, Desiderius Erasmus, Martin Luther, Philip Melanchthon, and John Calvin, to name only a few, all recognized that an education based on orthodox Christian theology created a fertile ground for Christian thinking to flourish in the minds of students. In pursuit of this goal, the church developed her own educational model—theologically sound and academically superior to anything contemporary educationalists have to offer—and developed Christian thinking in the minds of her youth.

This book is a call for Christian educators to abandon the impoverished pedagogies of the world and recover the rich educational heritage which was a living part of the church's schools until the recent past. A basic premise of this book is that all educational theory has a theological bias, and so it is important to make clear that I write this book as one who subscribes to the confessions of the Evangelical Lutheran Church which dictate that Scripture, as the infallible revelation of the Triune God, is the normative force for both theology and pedagogy. Academic disciplines such as philosophy, psychology, or sociology will naturally inform the educational philosophy of the church, but Scripture must remain the ultimate arbiter of issues such as truth, goodness, beauty, and the nature of man and his relationship to others. This confessional subscription also means that I possess the chronic Lutheran habit of looking at everything through the lens of Law and Gospel. The Law is everything in Scripture that speaks about our sin and God's wrath. The Gospel is everything that points to, and offers, forgiveness and grace in Christ. Rightly distinguishing between these two doctrines is not only the key to properly understanding Scripture and unlocking the saving truth of the Gospel, but it is crucial in determining the nature of education and the role it occupies in the mission of the church.

This is not a purely academic book. It is written from the perspective of a college professor who has taught students preparing to teach in Christian schools, a pastor who spent years catechizing young minds, a schoolteacher who struggled to develop a curriculum that was appropriate for a Christian school, and a father whose children have grappled with the issues raised in this book. It is written for any confessionally-minded Christian educator who has sensed that the supposedly unbiased, theologically neutral educational theories are not unbiased or neutral at all. I suspect more than a few teachers fit into this category. These are good, pious Christians who take their confession seriously and perceived that something was not quite right with the way they were taught to teach. At an intuitive level, they sense that the constantly revolving door of pedagogical theories and government-sanctioned curricula fall short of what they want to accomplish as Christian teachers. They know that it is not enough to have a religion class, a once-a-week chapel service, and a curriculum that simply avoids morally offensive material. At a gut level, these teachers know that Christian education is in need of an approach to teaching that is both radically different and always the same: radically different in that it deliberately and intentionally seeks to shape young minds to hold fast to the confessions of the church and to look to God in faith and their neighbor in love[1]; and always the same in that it continues the great traditions of Christian education that were developed over two millennia.

Despite the sometimes-harsh criticisms of the theories and methods of American education, this book should not be taken as an indictment against teachers. I do not think harshly of Christian teachers who are laboring under these theories. They were taught just as I was taught, and I would probably still be supporting those theories had it not been for seemingly serendipitous events like those I have described. And so it is especially to teachers that I extend a friendly invitation to join me on a journey to explore the theological implications of contemporary educational theory and to test some alternatives with the promise of an approach to teaching that really does prepare students to think as Christians.

Part I

Bitten by the Snake

How Theology Shapes Pedagogy

Currently in colleges of education across America, almost all future teachers learn from a standard canon of educational thinkers whose work forms the basis for the goals, methods, and structure of the modern American classroom. When students are introduced to these educationalists, there is rarely, if ever, any consideration given to what they believed or confessed in their personal lives. This is radically different from how the church has traditionally measured teachers. Up to the twentieth century, theology has always been the measuring stick for all other areas of knowledge. This was especially true for education. A teacher's confession of faith was always considered to be the first criterion in judging whether or not his or her teaching was acceptable. In the sixteenth century, the influential Lutheran educator, Valentin Trotzendorf, insisted, "Those who belong to our school, let the same also be members of our Church and those who agree with our faith, which is most sure and true; because of perhaps one godless person out of the whole body, some evil happens."[1] Today, however, we are told that what teachers believe and confess has little or nothing to do with the methods they advocate. According to this principle, education can be structured purely according to a researcher's scientific theories and principles with little regard to what they believe and confess.

This approach is a legacy of the nineteenth and twentieth centuries, which presented the image of the dispassionate scientist in a white lab coat as the ideal model: one who carried out research without any consideration of personal biases or theological opinions. The assumption is that research, including educational research, is a matter of scientific discovery alone, of studying everything in an "atheological" way; as though a scientist's personal confession has no bearing on what he or she observes or teaches. But is it truly possible for a scientist to operate in this way? I argue that it is not. A researcher's personal beliefs, to one degree or another, will affect his or her research, coloring the observations and shaping the conclusions. For example, if a scientist refuses to believe that the flood occurred as described in Genesis 6–9, then he or she will not consider the effects of that flood on nature, geography, or the development of civilization.[2]

If this is true for the so-called "natural sciences," it is certainly also true for psychology and sociology. Research in these behavioral sciences will always be influenced by what the investigator believes, teaches, and confesses. Very often, justification for the latest educational fads open with the familiar "Research has shown…" These words tend to silence debate and are regarded as normative by the educational community, implying that there can be no room for theological criticism. Such normative "research-based" education has dominated teacher formation now for close to a century. Over that time, there have been countless studies about a particular pedagogical method over and against another. The educational world is awash with trendy pedagogies, each promising to increase student learning or improve student engagement. Project Based Learning, Daily Five, and Educational Grit are but a few examples. Growth Mindset promises to alter children's internal voice by using positive thinking and affirming language and actions. For the latter, a website advocates that teachers engage students in "Grow-ga," an exercise that pairs yoga with positive affirmation.[3] The movement has spawned an entire industry of consultants, advocates, and resource supplies. Encouraged by professional educrats, teachers can build their expertise in this field through professional development courses that are accompanied by instructional manuals, classroom posters, videos, books, charts, journals, calendars, t-shirts, coffee mugs, and wine glasses.

One would assume that, with all this research (and the billions of dollars that have funded it), education would have made enormous progress and students would be smarter than ever before. Surely after a century of researching the optimal educational environments and ideal teaching methods, the educational establishment should be able to point to some measurable improvement. Students today, who have been the beneficiaries of such prodigious research, should be better read, more thoughtful in their discourse, wiser in their deliberations, and more intent on pursuing the virtuous life. However, in considering the vulgarity that permeates popular culture, and the level of civic and political discourse exhibited in recent elections, one would be hard pressed to make the case that funding all this educational research has been money well spent.

So why has this approach failed? Perhaps it is because we have never asked the fundamental question, "What does the researcher teach, believe, and confess?" In response to the argument "Research has shown…", I would argue that very often the research reveals more about the researcher than the subject matter. Indeed, a researcher's personal beliefs about such things as the nature of man, the nature of God, the reality of sin, how we know truth, and so on, influences how he or she approaches education. For example, if I reject that children are born as sinful people, then I will look for some other explanation to justify their bad behavior. I will probably be inclined to remove the blame and guilt from the child and place it on the family, society, or religion. Or, if I believe that God is not the author of truth, goodness, and beauty, then I will look elsewhere for the source. I might well be inclined to believe that children construct their own truth, and so my research will revolve around proving that belief.

The point is this: what educational philosophers believe and confess dictates not only the questions they ask, but the answers they arrive at. As fundamental as this is, the beliefs of the educational thinkers are rarely, if ever, considered in educational circles. Future teachers are exposed to the theories of these educationalists and are shown how to apply them, but are never forced to confront the origins of those theories. They are given the 'what,' but not the 'why.'

I will demonstrate that beliefs and practices are inextricably linked, and I will show that an educational model cannot be uncritically used without importing the belief system upon which that model is constructed. This is not to imply that everything that these educationalists observed or suggested was wrong or should be rejected. Often one finds similar methods suggested by approved Christian pedagogues. However, without knowing the theological biases of these educational philosophers, no teacher can properly distinguish between what is usable and what is detrimental.

The Twentieth Century Educationalists:
A Case of Snakes in Sheep's Clothing

In the American educational community, it is widely accepted that Christian theology should have little to say about educational methods. In some cases, Christian educators may include Christian content, but the basic pedagogical theories and methods are generally taken from what is current practice in government-run education. It is also widely accepted that teachers should look first to child and adolescent psychology as the driving force of all pedagogy. These principles are relatively new to the field of education and were imposed in the late nineteenth and early twentieth century by those who wished to prevent the church from exercising her historic mission of teaching children. The result has been a complete paradigm shift. The church, with her 2000 years of educational experience, had produced some of the most enduring and insightful educational thinkers of all time. Now, however, she has been stripped of any influence on pedagogy, while the very young (and relatively inexperienced) field of the social sciences enjoys complete autonomy to take its place as the driving force behind current teaching methods.

This shift was partly driven by the scientific revolution, which saw science as the key to man's future. Previously, truth, goodness, and beauty were the central points of focus for the church's pedagogy—the great standards for which every student was to strive. In contrast to current standards set by government educators—things like test scores or nebulous learning outcomes—these were regarded as transcendent and eternal, aspects of God manifested independently of time and culture. If students were to fully appreciate the work of God, they also had to understand truth, goodness, and beauty. We will return to these standards in more detail later. Driven by the apotheosis of science, educators slowly abandoned the teaching of these standards in favor of an empirical approach to knowledge, reflecting the belief that science was the only trustworthy way of understanding the world.

From the days of the great educator and theologian Augustine of Hippo (A.D. 354-430) to the early nineteenth century, education was recognized to be the church's mission. Education was about understanding truth, and for the church, truth was transcendent; that is, it came not from within the individual, but from Christ who claimed to be "truth made flesh." In his work "On Christian Doctrine" Augustine famously said,

> Let every good and true Christian understand that wherever truth may be found, it belongs to his Master; and while he recognizes and acknowledges the truth, even in their religious literature, let him reject the figments of superstition, and let him grieve over and avoid men who, when they knew God, glorified him not as God, neither were thankful; but became vain in their imaginations, and their foolish heart was darkened.[4]

For centuries, the church had entrusted the task of teaching to sound Christian pedagogues who recognized Christ as the author of all truth.

In the 1500s, the Reformers recognized that, in order to grasp Evangelical theology, a child's mind must be trained in a complementary way. While the changes made to education were dramatic and set the stage for modern public education, an indisputable union was maintained between the church and school. In speaking of university reform, Luther affirmed this principle:

> I would advise no one to send his child where the Holy Scriptures are not supreme. Every institution that does not unceasingly pursue the study of God's word becomes corrupt.... I greatly fear that the universities, unless they teach the Holy Scriptures diligently and impress them on the young students, are wide gates to hell.[5]

The Enlightenment

The Enlightenment began chipping away at the bond between the church and education. By the nineteenth century, there were educators who believed that this bond was detrimental to a proper education. The famous educational reformer, Johann Pestalozzi (1746-1827), argued that children should not look to the church for correct doctrine, but to themselves. He said, "Believe in yourself, O Man—believe in the inner meaning of your being. Then will you believe in God and immortality." According to Pestalozzi, traditional catechetical teaching done by the pastor hindered healthy spiritual development. He argued, "Surely the best catechism is the one the children understand without their pastor."[6]

Friedrich Froebel (1782-1852) took this one step further. He believed that Christian doctrine corrupted children, and so it was necessary for them to be removed from the influence of the church and their parents at an early age before they became "infected" with an unhealthy understanding of God. Until the time of Froebel, children generally enrolled in school at age seven. Froebel wanted to start them earlier so that they could be properly trained by "approved" teachers in a new "world religion" that would enable them to rise above confessional boundaries and see that all religions were the same. Froebel stated, "Education guides man to understand himself, to be at peace with Nature and to be united with God."[7] The name he gave to this new early childhood program of indoctrination was Kindergarten. The concept was rejected by his countrymen in Germany, but some years later it would be warmly received in America. Having been freed from the guiding principles of Christian doctrine, education could now be molded according to any number of theological and worldviews.

The dominant worldview among twentieth-century educationalists was one that embraced evolution—not just the evolution of species, but also social evolution in which man and society progressed toward a perfect world. While today we most often associate evolution with Charles Darwin, in the late nineteenth century, the writings of Herbert Spencer (1820-1903) were perhaps more influential. While Spencer is relatively unknown now, in the second half of the nineteenth century he was one of the most discussed philosophers. Before Darwin wrote *The Origin of Species*, Spencer wrote about social evolution and coined the familiar phrase "survival of the fittest." According to Spencer, social perfection was not just possible, it was inevitable. To prove it, he combined evolutionary concepts with the new scientific field of psychology to demonstrate that mankind was progressing or evolving toward a superior culture, and that this evolutionary progress could be observed and directed through scientific experimentation. Spencer developed a child-centered model of education that was guided by the new science of psychology along with his evolutionary views. The result was the substitution of psychology for theology as the standard by which all educational practice was to be measured. By this new measurement, the education of the past, which had been concerned chiefly with teaching truth and wisdom, and which Spencer viewed as irrelevant in view of the great strides man had made in modern times, was deemed wicked because it was "most often conducted by forcing irrelevant information into the minds of reluctant children by methods that were patently barbarous."[8] Spencer believed that "in education the process of self-development should be encouraged to the uttermost. Children should be led to make their own investigations, and to draw their own inferences. They should be told as little as possible and induced to discover as much as possible."[9]

Reflecting on his vision of social evolution, he says, "Humanity has progressed solely by self-instruction; and that to achieve the best results, each mind must progress somewhat after the same fashion, is continually proved by the marked success of self-made men."[10] Spencer's, Pestalozzi's and Froebel's ideas would inspire many of the twentieth-century educationalists. The church, with its long history of educational thought and methods that had been honed for over a millennium and a half, was discarded. Psychology was now king; and evolutionary theory, with its hope of perfection through continual improvement, was presented as the new savior of mankind.

The rejection of revelation as a basis for truth, the psychologizing of education, and the belief in social evolution had a decisive influence on those pedagogues who hold sway in today's colleges of education. Rather than attempt to explore every influential educationalist or school of thought used in teacher training programs, this book will instead focus on four of the most commonly studied educationalists: John Dewey, who is sometimes called the father of progressive education; Lev Vygotsky, who is best known for his theories of social constructivism; Maria Montessori, who was portrayed as a pioneer in early childhood education; and Jean Piaget, a psychologist who is known for his stages of cognitive development. This book will not present an in-depth critique of their educational theories, but will instead flesh out their theological views, including Secular Humanism and Marxism (Dewey and Vygotsky) and Gnosticism (Montessori and Piaget). It can be argued that the theories of Dewey and Piaget are no longer applicable and that most educational thinkers today value them only for their historical significance. While there is merit to this perspective, I would argue that the theological premises upon which their pedagogical ideas were built still remain. A careful reading of all these leading figures reveals that they approached their task with strong convictions about theology, science, psychology, and evolution. They were "true believers" with regard to their personal convictions, and they labored to use education to promote their beliefs—a goal they made no attempt to hide. While the educational community portrays these thinkers as atheological, there is, in reality, no such thing. Everyone has a theology, even it if is a denial of the existence of the divine. While the educational community may choose to ignore the theological views that shaped their pedagogy, the Christian cannot. Without sound Christian doctrine, one is not without theology, but simply at the mercy of theologies invented by limited, sinful human beings.

The Secular Humanists and Marxists

John Dewey (1859-1952)

John Dewey is widely acknowledged to be one of most influential thinkers in American education. Generated in the first half of the twentieth century, Dewey's ideas formed the foundation for much of today's educational theory. A philosopher by trade, Dewey has been called "Evolution's Philosopher" for his work in applying social evolutionary thought to modern philosophy. His goal was to embed secular humanism into the American psyche, and to a large extent, he succeeded.

Dewey, along with thirty-three other American intellectuals, signed a landmark document called *The Humanist Manifesto* (1933) which called for a complete overhaul of American institutions. From the signers' perspective, the twentieth century marked the beginning of a new era of progress toward universal harmony. They declared that "man's larger understanding of the universe, his scientific achievements, and deeper appreciation of brotherhood" had rendered old religions (primarily Christianity) outdated and irrelevant. They called for a new "religion" that was based not on a belief in a supernatural God who revealed wisdom to man (through Holy Scriptures), but one that would enable the intellectual powers of man to be released in order to discover the solutions for the world's problems. The manifesto called for replacing capitalism with a new socialist world order that would be a "free and universal society in which people voluntarily and intelligently cooperate for the common good." The doctrine of social evolution underpinned the whole document. It declared that "man is a part of nature and that he has emerged as a result of a continuous process."[11] It is most unfortunate that few education students have ever seen or heard of the *Humanist Manifesto* because many of the ideas that it puts forth are also fundamental to Dewey's educational model: Progressive Education.

While the term "Progressive Education" is not often used in contemporary educational courses, many of the concepts that form the staple for the methods used in the American classroom have their origin here. The model draws on many of the ideas that had been previously promulgated by the likes of Pestalozzi and Froebel, and is best understood in the context of a romantic view of childhood which was common among late 19th-century intellectuals in which children were seen to be naturally curious about all things. An ideal education, therefore, should allow them to learn in a natural way according to their own curiosities. A popular analogy from the time was that children were like flowers that, when planted in good soil, would naturally develop into good, strong, healthy, adults.[12]

Progressive education stresses that 1) children learn best from hands-on activity, 2) they should be allowed to discover what interests them the most, and 3) education should be oriented toward equipping children for "real-life" experience. Dewey states, "Education, therefore, is a process of living, and not a preparation for future living."[13]

This model elevates the teaching process above the quality of the material taught. According to Dewey, true education comes not by exposing children to the great works of civilization throughout the ages (music, art, literature, etc.), but "through the stimulation of the child's powers by the demands of the social situation in which he finds himself."[14] Thus teachers have the responsibility to carefully observe children, make note of their needs, and then develop a purposeful curriculum to address those needs. This was not simply about improving educational standards or classroom performance. Although educators throughout the centuries have always recognized the importance of these concepts, Dewey enshrined them as the all-important measurements—his Rule of Faith—for good education.

This was no simple matter of improving educational standards or classroom performance. Progressive education was an expression of Dewey's beliefs and a vehicle to reform society according to his particular confession of faith. In 1897 he wrote *My Pedagogic Creed*. This "creed" is divided into four articles and contains seventy-three statements of belief, each of which begins with "I believe..." For Dewey, this creed was as foundational to progressive education as the Apostles' Creed is to the Christian Church; and yet, like the *Humanist Manifesto*, few, if any, education students are aware of its existence.

My Pedagogic Creed calls for the rejection of all beliefs in a personal God in favor of a "logical" and "scientific" understanding of the world. According to Dewey, the world is on a great evolutionary path toward enlightenment. Traditional religion, with its doctrinal commitments and its trust in the providence of an all-powerful God, was not just outdated, it was a hindrance to the future progress of the world. For Dewey, Christianity was un-American and antidemocratic, terming it a "spiritual aristocracy." This "aristocracy" grew out of what he saw as an elitism embedded in Christianity's division between "the saved" and "the damned", its insistence on correct teaching, and its willingness to identify false teachers.[15] According to Dewey's confession, Christianity was preventing the realization of the universal brotherhood of man and a perfected world free from conflict. He wrote that the Christian religion "has been petrified into a slavery of thought and sentiment, as intolerant superiority on the part of the few and an intolerable burden on the part of the many."[16] Dewey also felt that it was impossible for a modern educated man to believe in historic Christianity because it had been thoroughly and resoundingly discredited by the modern science of evolution. Christianity had been hopelessly relegated to the dustbins of history for, as Dewey said, "Religion has lost itself in cults, dogmas and myths."[17]

Even though Dewey claimed to be an atheist, he still saw the value of a religious sentiment, which for him, was completely different than historical religions with their antiquated rituals and doctrines. What society needed was to demolish the musty, aging temple of religion and construct a new one in its place: one based on the individual and his or her own understanding of what was and was not religious. One had to choose one's own religious impulse—so long as this impulse did not direct one toward Christianity, with its doctrines, rituals and condemnation of false doctrine that marked it as far from true religion. Dewey held that established religions–by which he almost always meant the Christian religion–were detrimental to being religious because they grew out of primitive man's fear of the unknown. Dewey argued that modern man, thanks to the advances of science, should by now have outgrown those fears. He believed that science had unlocked the secrets of the universe and had taken religion's place as "the seat of intellectual authority."[18] The truly religious person was the one who was "repelled from what exists as a religion by its intellectual and moral implication."[19] Thus the religious impulse could spring from poetry, literature, a beautiful sunset or a well sung song just so long as it wasn't introduced by a formal religion. Dewey saw the value of these religious impulses as therapeutic, enabling people to feel better about themselves and what they were doing, as well as driving them to work for the common good of society.

Under Dewey's philosophy, the God of the Apostles' Creed became a tyrant–one who wills to keep man subservient, to keep him ignorant of the true nature of the world and condemned to a life of never realizing his full potential. Only the god of science, the god of philosophy–in short, the god which Dewey allowed to be worshipped–can free the individual and society to evolve and overcome its limitations. This is the theology behind progressive education. Dewey's child-centered methods were a direct effort to turn children away from a Christian concept of God and the corresponding reliance on His grace. Instead, children were to find within themselves the answers that life demanded. The Triune God was to be replaced with the god of self. This was Dewey's new orthodoxy.

It is remarkable that, while Dewey was quick to condemn Christianity as being un-American and anti-democratic, he was generous with his praise of education in the new Soviet Union. In 1928, he toured Russia with several other educators. Upon his return, he lavished praise on the new Soviet society. He wrote, "I have never seen anywhere in the world such a large proportion of intelligent, happy, and intelligently occupied children."[20] Presumably Dewey neglected to speak to any survivors of the infamous "Red Terror" in which the Bolsheviks slaughtered hundreds of thousands of their fellow countrymen. Perhaps the lavish praise heaped upon him by his Soviet hosts colored his view. To them, Dewey was one of the revolution's "most renowned writers." The Communists had adopted his Progressive education model as the basis for a new Soviet pedagogy that trained children to reject religion, replaced classical studies with worker-friendly technical studies, and rejected the established authority of church and state in favor of the authority of the collective. Dewey felt that this new Soviet approach to education should serve as a role model for the integration of his reforms in America. He wrote,

> While an American visitor may feel a certain patriotic pride in noting in how many respects an initial impulse came from some progressive school in our own country, he is at once humiliated and stimulated to new endeavor to see how much more organically that idea is incorporated in the Russian system than in our own.[21]

What drew Dewey's admiration about the Russians was their recognition of the incompatibility between classical studies and their new world order. This is what lies at the heart of the conflict between the Christian confession and Progressive education. Classical studies emphasize the importance of languages, respect for wisdom, and a contemplative reflection of one's life. Since the days of St. Augustine, the church has recognized that, as children were trained in these things, they would be well prepared to understand the Christian faith. Such an education enabled children to properly study the Word of God, look to it for truth and wisdom, and serve their neighbor with works of love. Dewey wanted a new religion, and he needed a corresponding form of education that would prepare children to receive this new faith with "glad and sincere hearts." In order for this to happen, education had to be reworked to awaken in students an awareness of their role in the social evolutionary process upon which Dewey based his religion. *My Pedagogical Creed* is peppered with terms like "social progress," "social consciousness," and "social growth." Dewey's insistence that children learn cooperatively grew from his desire to use schools as nurseries for this new brand of socialism. He said, "The best and deepest moral training is precisely that which one gets through having to enter into proper relations with others in a unity of work and thought."[22] In a progressive classroom, students would work cooperatively, trust only scientific research, and reject historical authority figures. They would form new moral constructs, solve social problems, and rise above religious differences, to create a utopic society marked by universal brotherhood. According to Dewey, the foundation of true education "comes through the stimulation of the child's power by the demands of the social situations in which he finds himself." Classical Christian education, which valued individual excellence, mastery of academic material, diligent study of history and literature, and deference to authority worked against Dewey's goals. He said, "The present educational systems, so far as they destroy or neglect this unity, render it difficult or impossible to get any genuine, regular moral training." According to Dewey, true education was "a process of living and not a preparation for future living."[23]

This process was to be the ethic of the new humanistic religion, and teachers were to be its chief proselytizers. They were the new social priests who had been given a near-divine call to maintain "proper social order" and see to it that children were directed in the right paths of "social growth." Dewey intentionally used scriptural terms to describe the role of the teacher in teaching this new faith. He declared "I believe that in this way the teacher always is the prophet of the true God and the usherer in of the true kingdom of God.... I believe that every teacher should realize the dignity of his calling; that he is a social servant set apart for the maintenance of proper social order and the securing of the right social growth."[24]

As a formal model of education, Progressive Education was most influential in the first half of the 20th century among the educational elites; however, with the onset of the Cold War, the Space Race with its emphasis on the hard sciences, and the counter-cultural movement of the 1960's, it fell out of favor and was replaced by other more "progressive" models.[25] In spite of this decline, many of the core tenets had embedded themselves within the colleges of education and were incorporated into subsequent educational models.

Lev Semyonovich Vygotsky (1896-1934)

Educational psychologist Lev Vygotsky has garnered a great deal of attention by North American educationalists in the last 40 years. Educators praise his insight on how children learn, his theories on language development, and his innovative methods. He is often held up as a revolutionary psychologist who was largely forgotten in his own country. Some have called him the Mozart of Psychology.[26] Virtually every student studying to be a teacher in America is introduced to his theories and methods.

For all the attention given to Vygotsky, few students learn about his background and motives. Surprisingly, many professors of education are unaware that Vygotsky was a Marxist/Leninist educator working in revolutionary Russia, or that he was one of the most influential educationalists under Josef Stalin, or that his life's work was the application of Marxist principles to education.[27] What is also seldom mentioned in educational literature is that Vygotsky's aim was to use education to create a new Soviet man who would work with his comrades to construct the perfect Communist state.

Vygotsky graduated with a law degree from the University of Moscow in 1917. Like Karl Marx, he was strongly influenced by Spencer's social evolutionary ideas. He believed that the Communist Revolution was part of the natural progress of social evolution. He imagined a new order being built on socialist principles that would eliminate all inequality, injustice, exploitation of workers, and, once and for all, the ruling structure of church and state. Vygotsky believed that, in order for the socialist state to succeed, it needed a pedagogy that was structured around the principles of Marxist psychology. Far from a dispassionate observer of human nature, Vygotsky was dogmatically committed to his Marxist philosophy, which he believed could be relied upon to shape a person's research. He said, "Marxist psychology is not a school amidst schools, but the only genuine psychology as a science. A psychology other than this cannot exist. And the other way around: everything that was and is genuinely scientific belongs to Marxist psychology."[28] So much for unbiased research.

Even though Marxism is not a religion, Christians would do well to consider it in theological terms. Indeed, this is the way that early Marxists looked at their philosophy. The Russian Marxist Anatoly Lunacharsky (1875-1933), [29]who was the Soviet Union's first People's Commissar of Education, believed that socialism was the new religion which would free people from the troubles of this world and inspire the development of a divine earthly kingdom. In his view, Marx was a religious genius on par with Isaiah, Jesus, and St. Paul.[30] In place of God, Marxists installed man, though certainly not man as a Christian would recognize. This Marxist vision of man is not a selfish, self-centered, sinful being, or as Luther put it, "man as so curved in upon himself that he uses not only physical but even spiritual goods for his own purposes and in all things seeks only himself."[31] Indeed what sort of God would that be? Rather, the Marxists invented a fictitious, perfected man who, having been liberated from the agents of oppression, was now free from such selfishness. In place of heaven, they promised a new earth where, having thrown off the shackles of money, property, and individuality, mankind would coexist in a blissful, classless society. Of course, this vision must ignore the tens of millions who were robbed of their property, sent to labor camps, and senselessly slaughtered to make way for all of this, not to mention the untold number of Christians whose churches were confiscated, and who were imprisoned, tortured, and martyred for not submitting to this new world order.

According to Vygotsky, truth was found in the worker. Inspired by Marx's theory of dialectic materialism, he believed that truth is social—it comes from a child's social interactions with others. Family, economic status, religion, and culture were all tools that children used to construct meaning. If those structures were deemed to be oppressive, which Vygotsky happily concluded they were at the time, then the reality constructed by children would undermine their ability to take their rightful place in the world. Remove those "oppressive" structures, and children would be freed to create new meaning and evolve along with society toward the new Marxist world order that would be populated with the new Soviet man.[32]

In this new Marxist psychology, there was no room for God or the ancient principle that truth, goodness, and beauty came from Him. Though he himself had received a classical education, Vygotsky believed that the old educational system was corrupt. He argued that it was merely a means for propping up the ruling elites who used their education to promote a version of truth, morality, and wisdom designed to oppress the working class. Chief among those elites was the church, which had imposed an unacceptable version of truth and morality upon society for far too long. He claimed that Christian morality was merely part of the "bourgeois morality" which was "fully laden with hypocrisy and mendacity." According to Vygotsky, by "preaching the Kingdom of God after death," the church had "implanted a kingdom of enslavers in the world." In the Marxist view of the world, Christian morality was "full of lies and hypocrisy" and had to be done away with. Vygotsky believed that a new era had dawned in which the new Soviet man, whom Vygotsky was helping to create, was "exploding the very foundations of Christian morality from within." Indeed, he rejoiced that, with the revolution, the "thousand-year link between morality and religion has been broken" and that "morality is beginning to acquire an increasingly temporal character."[33]

In the new Marxist classroom, students would not learn from a well-educated teacher about truth, goodness, and beauty; nor would they study Latin, theology, classical philosophy, or classical literature. All these things were deemed to be of no use in the new world order. Instead, students would learn to be productive, efficient, cooperative workers through a practical polytechnical education. Furthermore, teachers were not to be viewed as authority figures who had mastered the subject material to be taught, but facilitators who encouraged children to discover and learn collectively and socially, and guided them to a deeper understanding of what the collective had determined to be of worth.

This gave rise to Vygotsky's famous theory of Zones of Proximal Development (ZPD). This theory is drilled into virtually every education student as a staple of their formation as a teacher and has come to dominate the educational world. Some suggest that ZPD is so fundamental to a child's development that parents need be familiar with it to properly raise their toddlers.[34] ZPD is defined as the gap between what a child comfortably knows and what they can only know with help. In order to move children to greater knowledge, the teacher's task is to provide learning structures or "scaffolds" to help them work cooperatively with their peers in order to master the new skill or knowledge. An effective teacher need only be a keen observer of a student and be able to provide an appropriate scaffolding for that particular student to use in order to progress through different levels of learning. At first glance, this seems to be common sense; however, there is more to Vygotsky's theory than meets the eye.

Vygotsky viewed a classroom as a socialist collective in which children were awakened to their new life as the working class as they became conscious of their economic struggles. In this environment, they learned best from their peers: their comrades, so to speak. It was imperative for children to conform to the will of the collective, and not defer to any higher authority, such as the teacher. Vygotsky understood his ZPD theory as a crucial tool for shaping young minds, who would then reject capitalist culture and religious morality. In place of these old structures of oppression was a new collectivism modelled by teachers who were to be regarded as peers of the students themselves. Children looked to other children for a behavioral standard that "originates from everyone, from the group."[35] Vygotsky's ZPD theory was not about a teacher directing students in their learning. It was about the social group moving a child to appropriate constructions of reality. It was about the group pressuring the individual to achieve conformity to the collective morality. It was about children surrendering their independence and their individuality. Thus, group work was to be praised and individual excellence was to be discouraged. It was not important for children to master the material that was traditionally required to be a well-educated person, nor was it important that they be taught to look to God in faith and be trained in matters of truth, goodness, and beauty. Such an education did not serve the new Marxist world order.

Vygotsky recognized that there would be times when a child's behavior was not in line with the interests of the group. In such cases, the teacher was to help the child see "the value of changing the way he behaves so as to accord with the interests of the group."[36] Routines should be designed to see that the child would be "in step with the group" and forfeit any claim to being right over and against the needs of the group. Gone from the Vygotskian classroom was a wise and virtuous teacher who was responsible for teaching that which is true, noble, right, pure, lovely, admirable, excellent, or praiseworthy (Phil 4:8). In its place, Vygotsky presented a teacher whose task it was to make sure children worked together in one happy collective, striving toward a Marxist-inspired world of harmony and tranquility.

If Vygotsky's ideas were so antithetical to American and Christian education, why were they not rejected from the outset? Why would America–a nation built on freedom and liberty, and forged by capitalism–want its teachers studying communist pedagogy? Why would Christian schools–which depend on the teaching of the revealed Word of God and regard teachers to be representatives of God's authority—want to promote social constructivism and the anti-authoritarianism of socialism?

After Vygotsky's death in 1934, his works were mostly forgotten in his own country. However, they were taken up with enthusiasm by American educators. In 1962, his *Thought and Language* was published with almost all references to Marxism and Leninism deleted from the translation.[37] It laid the groundwork for another translation, *Mind In Society*, published in 1978. This work was well received by American intellectuals, who quickly sought to uncritically incorporate Vygotsky's ideas into American educational training. Thus, at a time when the Soviet system, which Vygotsky help create and maintain, was just about to crumble under its own spiritual, ideological, and economic bankruptcy, his works were being welcomed into the very system that Vygotsky thought to be so utterly and irredeemably corrupt.

Vygotsky's ideas continue to thrive. Under names like "liberatory pedagogy," "critical pedagogy," and "emancipatory pedagogy," he has become the hero of a new generation of neo-Marxists who see the dialectic struggle not in terms of the ruling bourgeois versus the worker, but as Western/Christian culture verses various oppressed sexual, economic, linguistic, or ethnic minorities. Under the guise of critical thinking, one author says, "children are to be taught to ask 'which (raced and gendered) social class groups and communities win and lose through particular policy and processes', and be taught about Marxist analysis and the class exploitative nature of capitalism." They are to "address and value ecological literacy and a readiness to act for environmental justice as well as economic and social justice." Teachers are to "ensure that schools' curriculum and the 'hidden curriculum' are anti-racist, anti-sexist, anti-homophobic." And educators are encouraged to develop a new "hidden curriculum" that advances a Marxist world view by addressing, identifying, critiquing, and combating "social class exploitation under capitalism, and its attendant class discrimination.[38] And you thought that Johnny was going to school to read, write, and learn arithmetic!

For these neo-Marxists, the church's close ties with the development of Western culture mark it as a repressive organization. Capitalism is evil, and religion a means of oppression. Morality is a construct of the powerful. Even the insistence of proper English usage is just a way to keep the elites in power. It is better by far for the twenty-first-century teacher to get children to work together through collaborative learning, to ask leading questions, and to affirm whatever moral decisions the group makes. Sometimes this takes an almost surreal form. Kindergarteners in the state of Michigan are expected to "participate in collaborative conversations with diverse partners about *kindergarten topics and texts* with peers and adults."[39] These tenets are all taken directly from Vygotsky and, as any quick Google search will show, they form the bread and butter of contemporary American educational thought.

The Gnostics

Maria Montessori (1870-1952)

Most Americans first encounter Maria Montessori through one of the more than 4,000 schools that bear her name. Montessori schools are associated with caring, peaceful environments in which children engage with what interests them, at their own pace. Numerous Montessori schools explain their approach in this way: "Montessori education offers our children opportunities to develop their potential as they step out into the world as engaged, competent, responsible, and respectful citizens with an understanding and appreciation that learning is for life."[40]

Montessori, who was a physician, maintained that her methods were thoroughly scientific. She believed that, through careful observation of children, one could create the optimal learning environment. She used her "scientific" method to devise a child-centered approach to education in which the curiosity of the child was paramount.

Montessori-educated children are taught to make choices regarding what they learn, believing that they learn best what interests them the most.[41] Hands-on, activity-based learning is lauded, and instead of looking to the teacher for direction, children are encouraged to learn from their peers through collaborative play.

Montessori's ideas have spread far beyond the walls of Montessori schools. Her methods are a standard part of teacher training and are especially influential in the field of early childhood education. Her theories on how young children learn have not only shaped the fundamental ways pedagogues understand children, but were also strong influences on Piaget and Vygotsky. In teachers' colleges across America, Montessori is presented as a ground-breaking pioneer, whose methods and theories are taught to future teachers with little regard for the radical theological goals that she had in mind.

While Montessori is often spoken of as a devout Roman Catholic, her teachings place her at odds with historic Christian doctrine.[42] Like most Enlightenment-inspired pedagogues, she rejected that children were born in sin and were in need of a Savior. Correspondingly, she rejected the doctrine that only in Christ is one able to perform spiritually good works. Instead, Montessori regarded children as not only innocent, but innately holy, even possessing divine redemptive qualities.

In describing the spiritual development of children, Montessori referred to them as "spiritual embryos" and "spiritual energies" that were seeking expression in a physical body.[43] If these "spiritual embryos" were properly nurtured, their divine nature would be freed to act as agents for the divine redemption of the world. In other words, children would be the ones to usher in an era of global peace and tranquility. Montessori writes, "It was Christ who showed us what the child really is…the adult's guide to the kingdom of heaven."[44]

According to Montessori, redemption was not salvation from sin, everlasting death, and the power of the devil. Writing in the wake of the European wars, she saw redemption as a temporal salvation: the earthly progression toward a new era in which people would live together in selfless harmony without wars and conflicts.

What is the evidence for this new plan of salvation? Historically, the Christian church has affirmed that God's plan of salvation is made known only through Christ and revealed to the world through the Holy Word of God. Not so for Montessori. According to her, Christ's words in Scripture could only be understood metaphorically at best. If one wanted to see God's plan of salvation being worked out in the world, one needed to observe children who were, after all, endowed with a measure of divinity. She wrote,

> The child then promises the redemption of humanity, and we might say that this truth is represented by the mystical symbol of the Nativity. The child must no longer be considered as the son of man, but rather as the creator and the father of man, point the way to a better life and bringing us light. The child should be regarded as…the father capable of creating a better humanity. It is incumbent upon us, therefore, to serve the child and create an atmosphere that can satisfy his needs.[45]

This salvation was all part of a divine evolutionary view of redemption. Redemption came not through Christ's perfect life and His all-sufficient death on the cross, but through a divine evolutionary process in which human beings had an active role. She wrote, "our proud civilization and all the marvelous achievements of evolution have been made possible by the self-sacrifice of humble saviors of whose work we are unconscious."[46]

This is why it was so important for children to explore their interests and look to their peers, not their teachers, for guidance. These were spiritual, divine beings who needed to be freed from the restrictions of education in order to be masters of their own learning. A classical curriculum, which trains the mind according to wisdom and stresses the importance of quality content, hindered a child's development. The teacher who gave unnecessary direction or instruction to children was, in effect, preventing their spiritual embryos from fully developing, thus hindering the advancement toward perfection and, in turn, preventing them from advancing this divine evolving plan for the cosmos. She wrote,

> The child whose attention has once been held by a chosen object, while he concentrates his whole self on the repetition of the exercise, is a delivered soul in the sense of the spiritual safety of which we speak. From this moment there is no need to worry about him - except to prepare an environment which satisfies his needs, and to remove obstacles which may bar his way to perfection.[47]

More will be discussed about the influence of Gnosticism on modern education later in this book; however, at this point, a brief explanation is necessary, for Maria Montessori was very much a Gnostic. In the first four centuries, the church battled against the heresy of Gnosticism (from the Greek word "to know"). Gnosticism held to a dualistic view of human nature in which the inner spiritual self was in conflict with the physical world. Salvation came when this spiritual self was enlightened to a knowledge of its true divine nature and thus escaped the confines of the material world. The early church condemned Gnosticism as a heresy because it denied salvation through Christ alone. As is the case with any compelling heresy, Gnosticism did not fade away in the fourth century, but persisted through the centuries to re-emerge as the heart of Maria Montessori's educational model.

Montessori's Gnostic theology was to be the vehicle that propelled the world to a new utopian age: a time when all wars and conflicts would cease and all would live together in universal brotherhood. One cannot but be struck with the complete failure of such a vision. The world remains a violent place, filled with conflict and self-centeredness, even among those who were educated in Montessori schools. To the Christian, this comes as no surprise. Montessori, like so many other secular pedagogues, denied the truth of original sin, which will forever pit mankind against God and against one another.

Jean Piaget (1896-1980)

It is difficult to overstate Jean Piaget's influence on the American educational landscape. His theories on child development and how children know (epistemology) have shaped teachers' understanding of the educational process in dramatic ways. While many in the psychological world regard Piaget as little more than a figure of historical interest, and while his influence in child development theory has waned, his educational theories continue to be taught in colleges of education across North America.

Piaget is most noted for two things: his theory of cognitive development and, related to it, something he called "genetic epistemology." Piaget believed that children progressed through a series of four predetermined stages of cognitive development in which they constructed their own knowledge by giving meaning to things around them. Of interest to our discussion is that, for Piaget, knowledge did not come from outside the individual. It did not originate with God and was not taught to students by a teacher. Knowledge was constructed by the child him- or herself. The important word here is "construct" because, according to Piaget, the key to children's development was not that they had sound teachers who taught what was wholesome or beneficial for a godly life, but that they were allowed to construct their own understanding of the world around them.

Like Montessori, he stressed the importance of letting a child's curiosity direct learning. He argued that children should be given every opportunity to explore, experiment, and experience learning with minimal direction or instruction from the teacher. Piaget backed up his theories with lab-like observations about how, what, and when children learn.[48] It is widely believed that Piaget's theories are based on sound scientific research. His followers portray him as the consummate objective social scientist, reporting only that which he observed, tested, and verified.[49] There is virtually no discussion of what he believed or confessed. In fact, Piaget had very clear theological opinions.

Piaget's father, who was a professor of Medieval Literature, was indifferent towards Christianity. His mother, however, was a devout Reformed Christian. When Piaget was a young man, she was concerned about his spiritual leanings and enrolled Piaget in a religion course. He dropped out, finding Christian theology difficult to reconcile with his views on biology—his true interest. The conflict between science and religion came to its resolution in Piaget when he found a copy of *Outlines of a Philosophy of Religion Based on Psychology and History* by Louis-Auguste Sabatier. Sabatier was a liberal mystic theologian who believed that in order to have a right understanding of God, one should not start with Scripture or the teachings of the church, but with "the religious impulse," which could be understood through the science of psychology. Psychology, not Scripture, was the proper means of understanding God. This was to be the first of two profound insights that shaped Piaget's understanding of God and religion.

The second came through Piaget's introduction to the ideas of French philosopher, Henri Bergson, who was the great opponent of Cartesian dualism and wrote a book called *Creative Evolution* in which he tried to harmonize evolutionary science with religion. According to Bergson, God was not a transcendent being who created the world and everything in it. Rather, God was a "vital energy" living within each person. This immanent god was just one part of a grand evolutionary movement that encompassed society, religion, knowledge, and biology. Bergson's idea inspired Piaget to develop a completely different understanding of what constituted god. God was not to be understood as a transcendent being who stood apart from his people revealing truth and wisdom, intervening in their lives for their good. Piaget maintained that psychology and sociology had exposed the illusion of such a god and had "destroyed classical theology."[50] God interacted with people only from within. Piaget said, "God is not a being who imposes himself on us from without. His reality consists only in the intimate effort of the seeking mind."[51] It is important to note that Piaget was not denying the existence of God, nor was he saying that he was a product of the human imagination. God did indeed exist, but knowledge of him, his reality, and his truth were found only in the workings of the biological mind. To Piaget, this was revolutionary. In his old age he said,

> I recall one evening of profound revelation. The identification of God with Life itself was an idea that stirred me almost to ecstasy because it now enabled me to see in Biology the explanation of all things and of the Mind itself.[52]

What was the nature of this god? To answer that, Piaget relied on a seventeenth-century German philosopher, Gottfried Leibniz (1646-1716). Leibniz is well-known for his work in mathematics; in fact, many contend that he invented calculus. He was a rationalistic Lutheran who sought to come up with a more philosophically acceptable understanding of the nature of God. He drew on ancient Gnosticism and maintained that the universe was made up of immaterial divine-like beings. The Monad is the one absolute being, and it has emanations called "aeons." The Monad with its aeons is indivisible and has no parts: it is the very essence of all things, divine in that it is beyond all words, doctrines, names, and thought itself. It is the eternal entity responsible for everything that exists.

Piaget married this Gnostic concept of the Monad to mysticism, creating a philosophical/gnostic spirituality which understood God as dwelling in biology, and the self being the place where truth and wisdom was found. Inspired with a missionary-like zeal, he said "at that moment I decided to consecrate my life to the biological explanation of knowing."[53]

Some will argue that these theological views were from Piaget's youth and therefore have little bearing on his later work. However, not only did Piaget *not* repudiate them, but, after gaining fame and notoriety for his child development theories, he repeatedly referenced his gnostic understandings in his later works. In his later years, Piaget praised the Gnostic Gospels, works that the church had declared to be heretical, as works of truth that the orthodox church had deliberately suppressed. He rejected the Christian teaching that men were sinful from birth, claiming that orthodox Christianity held to the error that "a chasm separates humanity from its creator." He asserted, "The Gnostics contradicted this. They held that self-knowledge is knowledge of God; the self and the divine are identical."[54]

Piaget's views on child development can only be understood in light of his theology. His cognitive development theory was designed to advance his understanding of God, religion, evolution, and epistemology. But in spite of their centrality to his theories, Piaget's personal beliefs are virtually ignored by educational professors. I imagine that it would be of considerable embarrassment to the secularized educational and psychological establishment if it was shown that Piaget had a theological agenda.

How does this "biological god" shape one's view of education? Classically, the mind was related to the brain, but a firm distinction was maintained. The mind was part of the soul. Therefore, classical education sought to teach that which would be beneficial to the mind—things like virtue, beauty, and wisdom. According to Piaget, such classical concerns contributed little to the development of this new biological mind. A more important focus was to discover how children constructed truth, unlocking the ideal environment for their mystical connection with the inner god of their minds. Truth, wisdom, knowledge, and understanding come not from outside sources, such as Scripture or learned people of the past, but from the god within. Piaget had no interest in leading children to discover who they have been created to be in Christ Jesus, or in training them to understand themselves in terms of their God-given vocations. He had no interest in teaching children to deny themselves. The most important thing was that children be allowed to develop a knowledge of their inner true self which resided in the physical body but was not a part of it. It was the result of the working of the ancient Monad who used biology to create the self. Thus, the goal was that children should draw on this true self to construct their own understanding of the world which would then shape their knowledge of truth and moral goodness. In Matthew 8, Christ instructs that we should become like children looking to him and trusting in his mercy, grace, guidance, and protection from sin and every evil. Piaget would have considered this to be an assault on evolutionary biology. He believed that we should be evolving not toward a childlike state, but toward a mature biological mind that holds understanding and knowledge independent of the Triune God.

How does one know if a child has successfully developed this mature biological mind? It is quite simply by following Piaget's own philosophy: by measuring where the child is according to Piaget's own stages of development. One of the marks of the ancient Gnostic teachers is that they claimed to have a special knowledge that no one else had. Here, Piaget reveals his love of Gnosticism as he makes the audacious claim that he, with scientific precision, knew the mind of a child and understood exactly how it developed.[55]

Piaget's philosophy represents a disturbingly odd blending of theological mysticism, Gnosticism, and biological science. He contended that people can have an inner experience with God apart from the Word. In fact, worse than that, under Piaget's schema the Word of God is a hindrance to such an experience. Instead, it is by looking inward, and not to the Word, that Piaget believed one could come to a perfect knowledge of the divine and achieve harmony and an understanding of the true self. Over all of this was an evolutionary sentiment that this was the path to perfection. This was Piaget's version of spirituality. He believed that if education could be reworked according to his views of child development, then society at large would achieve a new balance. The world was still in the process of evolution. Society and mankind were progressing upward toward a higher noble plain and it was necessary to leave behind outdated concepts like sin, selfishness, ignorance, and strife. It was also necessary to replace the old classical traditions of education with new traditions that were based on this evolutionary, child-centered view. Far from being an objective scientist who merely reported what he observed, Piaget's work was all about building a system that would support his theological views. Using psychology and evolutionary theory, he replaced the transcendent God of the Christian faith with an inner god of the biological mind. He replaced the approved teachers of the past and the revealed wisdom of God as found in Scripture with a wisdom that was constructed by the mind itself. In place of hope in the life of the world to come, he presented the hope of a world perfected by our own doing.

Piaget's Cognitive Development and Fowler's Theory of Faith Development

Piaget's theological views were largely ignored by the psychological and educational communities that took up his ideas. That was certainly unfortunate, but worse was the silence of Christian educators and theologians about the nature of Piaget's views. This silence resulted in Piaget's theories being adopted by Christian educators who were eager to make the teaching of faith as respectable and modern as the latest trends in secular education.

Influential in this respect was the work of James Fowler who wrote the book, *Stages of Faith: The Psychology of Human Development and the Quest for Meaning* (1981). Fowler's Faith Development Theory applied Piaget's approach to the development of faith. Like Piaget, Fowler divided faith into distinct stages that represented the gradual progression or evolution of the individual toward the perfect or the universalizing faith. Fowler, following Piaget's lead, believed that faith could be scientifically observed and quantified. Therein was a basic conflict. Historically, the Christian church had defined faith not as a psychological response, but as a body of doctrines or beliefs confessed by the body of Christ and handed down to successive generations of Christians. In addition, the church had always confessed the unique role of the Holy Spirit in bringing a person to a saving relationship with the Triune God. This faith looked to the Word of God—not personal feeling—for truth. Fowler's solution to this conflict was to simply redefine faith. Using Piaget's schema, faith became a psychological phenomenon independent of and apart from a confession of faith. It became something that the individual constructed while moving through the various stages of life. Thus, for Fowler, the development of faith in a Muslim could be equal to that of a Hindu or a Christian. The content may vary from religion to religion, but the essential characteristics remained the same and could be measured by the psychological markers that had been determined by Fowler.

Fowler's approach was taught to a whole generation of pastors and teachers. It was incorporated into religious educational programs and curricular materials. It was presented as the way for Christian educators to describe faith so that it sounded respectable to the academic world and the psychological community. What counted now was not whether one believed, confessed, and taught the truth, but a child's "faith journey": his or her personal evolutionary path toward spiritual wholeness. With the acceptance of Faith Development Theory, Jean Piaget, the man who rejected the Triune God for a mystical god of the biological mind, was now being preached from pulpits and taught in Christian classrooms across America.

Conclusion

This chapter has looked at only four thinkers. Some might argue that they are not representative of what is currently taught in colleges of education. One could argue that there are other newer pedagogues who should be examined. There may be some merit to that argument; however, these four are still relevant for two reasons. First, they illustrate that there is no such thing as an unbiased scientific approach to educational theory. A study of other pedagogues would reveal that they all had theological agendas that shaped their observations and conclusions as well. This is a basic premise of this book. The question that the Christian educator, parent, and pastor must ask is this: Does that agenda help or hinder the formation of a student in the way of Christ? Second, their theological presuppositions have metastasized and spread throughout the educational world. Sometimes the influence is subtle; at other times it is obvious, but it is certainly present. Before considering alternatives for Christian education, it is important to examine how these alien theologies manifest themselves in contemporary educational theory and practice.

The Venom of Liberal Education

Each semester I used to ask my teacher education students, "What is the most important skill you want to teach children?" Without hesitation, they answer, "critical thinking." When I ask how they would teach critical thinking, they say, "By asking leading questions." "How does asking leading questions teach critical thinking?" I then ask. At this point I am met with puzzled stares. Wanting to drive home the point with my "leading questions", I ask, "And just what is critical thinking?" I have yet to be given a lucid answer. A few soon realize that, for all the talk they have heard in their courses about the importance of critical thinking, they have never learned how to think critically about so-called "critical thinking" itself. I suppose the idea is that asking leading questions means questioning the validity, accuracy, or relevance of something. But how helpful is that if you don't know how to find the answers to the leading questions, or explain them within the broader context of the Christian life?

The educational world is filled with buzzwords like "self-awareness," "differentiated instruction," "child-centered learning," "inquiry-based instruction," and my personal favorite, "brain-based learning" (as if there is learning which takes place without the brain) that are readily used by many Christian educators with little thought about what they mean and how they relate to Christian education. "Critical thinking" is one of these buzzwords. Who does not want students—especially Christian students—to think critically in a world in which they are confronted by so many competing ideas? We want them to be able to discern truth from lies, good from evil, and beauty from ugliness. One would assume that teaching children to think in this way would involve learning the basic tools of logic and rhetoric in order to strengthen their ability to reason and argue. It would also be most beneficial if they learned what the great thinkers of the past have said about critical thinking. But unfortunately, this is not the case.

The Uncritical Thought of Critical Thinking

Critical thinking is a key concept behind the educational paradigm that has come to dominate colleges of education in the West: liberal education. This is not to be confused with classical liberal arts education. Whereas a classical liberal arts education emphasizes the right use of one's freedom in service to one's neighbor, modern liberal education strives to free individuals from anything that hinders their attainment of personal happiness. This concept has its roots in the Enlightenment's quest to liberate the self so it can develop its potential on its own terms. Jean-Jacques Rousseau (1712-1775) is widely acknowledged to be the father of this type of thinking.[1]

It is hard to overstate how much Rousseau despised the classical liberal arts education model that the church had been using for centuries. In an essay "On the Moral Effects of the Arts and Sciences"[2] he claimed that the liberal arts corrupted people and that its recovery in the Renaissance multiplied all kinds of evil in society. It made people artificial in their dealings, vain, and more servile. He concluded that "our minds have been corrupted in proportion as the arts and sciences have improved."[3] Rousseau contended that the classical liberal arts existed only because of human vice. Astronomy was born of "hatred, falsehood, and flattery; geometry of avarice, physics of an idle curiosity and even moral philosophy of human pride."[4] The solution was for society to turn away from the liberal arts and the church which relied on the arts for educating her young, and to look to the self as the source for pure, untainted truth.

The opening lines of Rousseau's famous work, *The Social Contract* (1762), declare, "Man is born free, and yet we see him everywhere in chains. Those who believe themselves the masters of others cease not to be even greater slaves than the people they govern."[5] According to Rousseau and the generations of disciples who followed, man is inherently good. He is born without sin and has been corrupted by the evil institutions of society, the worst of which is the church. Furthermore, Rousseau believed that truth came not by the revelation of God, but from within each individual who, being inherently good, had an equal claim to truth and wisdom along with everyone else.

But those beliefs are contrary to the fundamental doctrines of the Christian faith. The church holds to the scriptural truth that children are born sinful. Truth, goodness, and beauty do not come from within, but from God. Christians are called to serve God and neighbor, not themselves. For this reason, the task of Christian educators is to mold children so that they deny the self and conform to the wisdom which comes from God.

How did Rousseau propose to address this obvious conflict of beliefs? It was by rejecting revelation as a reliable source of knowledge, jettisoning the concept of sin, and ridding education of Christian influence. He believed that if this could be done, teachers could begin molding children afresh according to their supposedly pure nature. In his educational work, *Èmile,* Rousseau argued that the purpose of education was to guide students through five stages of development so that they learn to reject religion with its inherent reliance on external wisdom and come to rely on their own natural impulses. If done properly, sometime around age twenty-five, students would attain the "Age of Happiness"—the point of being truly happy because they had learned to live by their own pure nature and not rely on the truth and wisdom found in others. They are liberated. He wrote, "Why should we build our own happiness on the opinions of others, when we can find it in our own hearts?"[6]

Rousseau apparently had a bit of difficulty discovering his own pure nature. His "natural impulses" caused him to recklessly engage in perverted sexual behavior and father several children out of wedlock—all of whom he abandoned and who died in foundling homes. One might think that this alone would disqualify Rousseau as an authority on how to educate and nurture children, but the educational establishment treats him as a true prophet of modern education.[7]

In Rousseau's writings, one finds the genetic code of liberal education and almost all contemporary pedagogical theories. They all rely on the same premises and share the same goal: the liberation of the student for the discovery of the true self. Students are completely free to decide what is true, good, and beautiful *for themselves.* This point is crucial to understanding what modern educationalists mean when they speak of critical thinking. In order to think critically, students must first reject everything—all pre-existing concepts of truth, goodness, and beauty, all that is understood as right and virtuous, any belief in personal sinfulness and forgiveness: in short, everything taught by church and family. Students then can begin to think critically about those concepts and adopt only the ones that best suit them and their understanding of life.

For the proponents of liberal education, anything that is opposed to critical thinking is classified as indoctrination—a term deliberately used to convey images of totalitarianism and the subjugation of the individual. As such, it is argued that indoctrination hinders a student from engaging in critical thinking. The fact that the term originally referred to the teaching of Christian doctrine and the process of catechesis is not lost on the advocates of liberal education. They consider the parents, pastors, and teachers who "force" children to learn from the historic confessions of the church to be the worst offenders.

Influential educational philosopher Meira Levinson argues forcefully for this position. Like Rousseau, she believes that the goal of all education should be complete autonomy or, as she calls it, "self-rule." To achieve this self-rule, students must follow a three-stage process. First, they must be taught to disassociate themselves from the truths and values with which they were raised. Second, they must independently and dispassionately evaluate those truths and values to see if they agree with them. Finally, they are then free to appropriate only those truths and values with which they agree.

Levinson believes that the most powerful agents working against a child's autonomy are parents and Christian schools. From her perspective, very often these authorities are tyrannically seeking to indoctrinate children in a predetermined set of values and beliefs that limit autonomy. With a fervor that would make any authoritarian dictator proud, Levinson argues that the best agency capable of freeing children from the oppression of such tyrants is government-run education, carefully structured around the principles of liberal education. She believes that only these schools are able to expose children to other values and perspectives and train them to regard all interpretations of reality and truth as equal.[8] This is the secret behind freeing children from a parental tyranny which would have them believe that there is only one correct understanding of what is true, good, and beautiful. While Levinson acknowledges that the state can also be tyrannical; when it comes to knowing what is best for a child, it is the state—not the parents nor the church—that is best suited to make that determination and allow children to develop "true personhood." Less parental involvement and more governmental control: this is social engineering plain and simple, and it is what Levinson regards as the ideal.[9]

For true believers in liberal education, this concept of autonomy is almost a sacrament that gives salvation: not a salvation from the spiritual oppression of sin, death, and the devil, but from the idea that sin, death, and the devil even exist. Adherents believe that biblical doctrines are mere constructs put in place to restrict children's liberty and retard their development. The promise is that if one drinks deeply of the sacrament of autonomy, he or she will enjoy a life of perfect freedom from the responsibility to others: the vocation of being a faithful husband or wife, a devoted child, a pious employer, a faithful worker, and the like. There would also be freedom from having to deny oneself, confess sin, and rely on the grace and mercy promised by a good and gracious God.

Levinson is not alone in her negative view of Christian education. University of Illinois professor, Walter Feinberg, argues that almost all education by religiously based schools is inconsistent with the "real" goal of education: autonomy. He claims that religious education is always in danger of being tyrannical and should be overseen by the government to ensure that children are not being overly indoctrinated in the values that the enlightened educationalist deems inappropriate.[10] Harvard Law School professor Elizabeth Bartholet argues that homeschooling is dangerous for the same reasons. After citing some extreme cases of children of survivalists—as if that is in some way typical of homeschoolers—she claims that homeschooling is a threat to American democracy, stating, "the issue is, do we think that parents should have 24/7, essentially authoritarian control over their children from ages zero to 18? I think it's always dangerous to put powerful people in charge of the powerless, and to give the powerful ones total authority."[11] Obviously liberal education encompasses a wide variety of views, and not all of them are as radical as those of Levinson, Feinberg, and Bartholet; however, very few, if any, within the educational establishment will voice support for an educational model designed to train children to be faithful, confessional Christians. There is near universal agreement that autonomy is the goal of all liberal education. This is the fulfillment of Rousseau's deepest desires.

As I was watching the construction going on outside my house while writing this, it dawned on me how liberating it must be to the man whose job it is to sit behind the controls of an excavator and fill dump trucks all day long. By virtue of his liberal education, he has been freed from the shackles of indoctrination which formerly bound him to his family, his community, and his church. His vocations, as worker, father, and husband are no longer sacred callings in which his purpose was to serve God by serving his employer and faithfully providing for his family. Now he should understand himself as a fully autonomous person who must create his own meaning of life that will be an expression of his new true personhood. Maybe he's not responsible for providing for his wife and children. Maybe he does not even need to be married. Maybe his obligations are getting in the way of his "true happiness." This selfish autonomy, which has been bestowed on him by the priests and priestesses of liberal education in government-sanctioned institutions, will advance him and the rest of society to a universal brotherhood of peace and tranquility. It is all rather silly.

Gnosticism and Education

Earlier we looked at how Gnostic ideas influenced people like Piaget and Montessori. In fact, Gnosticism has influenced educational philosophy well beyond these two thinkers. An explanation of the basic tenets of Gnosticism will be helpful prior to exploring the broader influence of Gnosticism on education.

Gnosticism is one of the earliest Christian heresies, with many of its teachings originating in ancient paganism. When Gnosticism came into contact with Christianity, it adopted Christian nomenclature, simulated the Christian sacramental system, and claimed new revelations of Christ.

According to Gnosticism, the universe began with an unknowable god called the "Monad." It is beyond all descriptions, names, categories, and human language: qualities that render redundant the rules of grammar and language. There are countless emanations of the Monad, called "aeons", and together they form the fullness of the divine, or the "pleroma". The "Monad" is the nurturer of the spiritual world, but not the creator of the material world.

One of the aeons is Sophia who represents true wisdom. According to many Gnostic myths, Sophia had a desire to be the spouse of the "Monad."[12] As a result she was cast out of the pleroma and gave birth to a ghastly monster-like god, the Demiurge, who was given the name "Yaltabaoth". This is the god who created the material world. He is an inferior god in that he is male, evil, capricious, and, at times, extremely violent. Gnostics consider him to be the god of the Old Testament. It was Yaltabaoth who subjected people to the constructs of a corrupt religion and a created world. Gnostics do not seek liberation from sin, but from ignorance of the true nature of the world. When they move from the dark, evil, material world into the world of light, immateriality, and pure spirituality, they achieve a *gnosis*—the special saving knowledge by which they know their real, genuine selves.

In traditional Gnosticism, Lucifer is neither regarded as evil nor the father of all lies. The only reason he is perceived in this way is because the Christian church has forced this construct on society. According to Gnostics he should be regarded more as a spiritual trainer or guru who works cooperatively with Christ, using temptations and trials to challenge people to break free of the material world.

Few educationalists, and even fewer teachers, understand or openly espouse Gnostic doctrine. However, Gnosticism has strongly influenced educational philosophies and methods. Gnostic thought plays an integral role in the philosophies of influential thinkers such as Jung, Hegel, Piaget, and Montessori. . Through them, Gnosticism has influenced many later educational theorists, most of whom are ignorant of this connection.

Gnostic doctrine has also entered educational theories through popular culture. In films like *Star Wars*, *The Matrix*, and *Harry Potter*,

Gnostic ideas are integrated into the storyline. In each of these films, some secret knowledge or wisdom is revealed to a neophyte by a guide or guru. The material world is generally portrayed as unreliable or evil or, perhaps, not even real. The acquisition of truth and wisdom does not require the discipline of learning grammar and logic, nor the careful study of the great writers of the past. It comes by getting in touch with the real wisdom that lies within each person.

For example, in *Star Wars*, Luke Skywalker is able to appeal to the inner goodness of his father despite the fact that Darth Vader spent his life serving darkness and is guilty of the ruthless slaughter of innocent lives. Vader's redemption comes not from a savior, but from listening to his guru (Luke) who can put him in touch with his "real self." Luke guides Vader out of darkness to a *gnosis* of the light and goodness that lies within. In *The Matrix*, Neo is led out of his ignorance by Morpheus so that he can see the material world for what it really is: a digital construct put in place to control people and blind them to reality.

Gnostic ideals permeate many children's movies. One example is the 2016 animated movie, *Trolls*. In classic fairytales, trolls are evil creatures who seek to deceive the innocent. The purpose of such tales was to teach children to be vigilant against deception, and to place their trust in the truth found in the Word of God. In this movie, however, trolls are cute and cuddly creatures who guide people to understand truth, goodness, and beauty. They are spiritual gurus guiding the ignorant to find meaning inside themselves. The chief of the trolls, Branch, declares "Happiness is inside all of us. Sometimes you just need someone to help you find it."[13] The message is that truth, goodness, and beauty don't come from the revealed Word of God or from the enduring wisdom of classical writers, but from looking deep inside oneself. The way to this inner truth is through a guide, one who has already been enlightened.

Because society has severed its connection with the objective standards of truth, goodness, and beauty as presented in Scripture, teachers and educationalists have become increasingly susceptible to such Gnostic ideals presented in film, television, music, and literature. Because their cultural markers are Gnostic in nature and convey a Gnostic worldview, those who shape the educational philosophy promoted in colleges of education will incorporate Gnosticism into

THE VENOM OF LIBERAL EDUCATION 37

their theories and methods without even being aware of it. The ideas that are presented on the screen, on the page, and in the music will inevitably trickle down into the classroom.

In *Gnostic America*, Peter Burfeind lays out a creed that is followed by many contemporary American cultural institutions.

> I am an absolutely free Self, born randomly in the body I have. My body—which is my position but is not essentially me—places me in a given situation in which I inherit certain values from my parents, from the church I grew up in, from my country, and from my culture. As I get older, I begin to break free from these values and, either I begin to discover who I really am, or I decide to create who I will be. I may have a crisis of identity at some point during this period, but I eventually must be me. This I do by making my own choices of what I will be, choosing my own politics, my own church, my own styles, my own music, my own sexuality, even my own gender; etc. Whatever it is that defines who I am, such things must be freely chosen by ME. I understand life as a journey whose paths are self-chosen. If there is some "out there" divine entity guiding me as I choose my path, it will communicate to me internally, personally. Along this journey, I may be assisted by certain gurus, both human or not so human. Or not.[14]

In the Christian church, the Apostles' Creed forms a dual function. It expresses the true doctrine of God and shapes the church into a confessing church. In a similar way, Burfiend's statements have an almost creedal standing in the educational world in that they shape the way many modern educationalists approach their task. Just as Christian theologians will search for corroborative evidence that supports the creeds of the church, so secular educationalists will look for evidence that will support their creedal position. The difference is that, while orthodox theologians are clear about their creedal positions, the educationalists feel no such compulsion. They deny that theories have a "theological" starting point and that much of the research is done with a bias toward their basic creedal position. Like every other creed, anything that contradicts it is generally deemed heretical and the one who holds to the "false teaching" is usually shunned lest his teaching infect the faithful. Thus, in colleges of education across America, there is little patience for those who hold to a different creed—say the Apostles' Creed—and who question the prevailing pedagogical paradigms. Those who do so are less likely to be hired, will not be granted scholarships, or will be denied research grants. In this way, the priesthood is kept pure and the central doctrines are kept whole and undefiled.

Like liberal education, Gnostic-influenced education regards the self as the source of truth, goodness, and beauty. When students are in touch with themselves, they have access to the unlimited potential of the pleroma. They don't need teachers, parents, and pastors because these authorities have been corrupted by their allegiance to an evil and materialistic god. In this ideology the ideal teacher is not one who is well-read or discerns what is useful and beneficial to intellectual, moral, and spiritual growth. Ideal teachers are regarded as facilitators (or gurus) whose chief task is to guide students to look inward and develop their own constructs of truth, goodness, and beauty. The result is that students are directed to endless group-work assignments and self-discovery assignments in the hope that they will be able to discover the wisdom that lies within themselves.[15]

It follows then, that with such a philosophy, it is of no use to teach students to master the rules of grammar, form letters properly, or build cogent arguments using established rules of logic which are based on absolute universal truth. Of course, this would equip them to study the great writers, poets, politicians, military leaders, and theologians who have shaped their world, but it would send the message that they should first look outside of themselves in order to be truly wise. Similarly, it would be counterproductive to train children to use the rules of grammar and logic in order to understand the true God as he is revealed through the Word. According to the Gnostics, this would only corrupt a child's ability to get in touch with the pleroma. They would rather have children ignorant of such things. In this way, children are better able to get in touch with their own inner wisdom, their own real world, and their own authentic selves.

It is somewhat antithetical to the nature of Gnosticism that a Gnostic would write a book on education. That would require using objective means (words) to convey what can only be known subjectively.[16] However, notable Gnostic, Samael Aun Weor, has written *The Fundamentals of Gnostic Education*. The parallels between what he proposes and what is taught in American colleges of education illustrate how Gnostic ideals have infiltrated contemporary educational philosophy. Weor calls for an outright rejection of parents and teachers as God-ordained authorities. To him, they represent oppression. He writes, "Our parents, teachers, tutors, authors, etc.—each one in his own manner—is a dictator." They are "dictators of the mind" that are as "widespread as weeds" and their goal is to "enslave" the mind and force it to live according to predetermined standards.[17] The priority of the enlightened teacher must be to protect children from being enslaved to the knowledge that others have determined to be of value, and free their minds and spirits to explore and experience truth for themselves. In the process, all forms of external discipline must be eradicated, because only then "does the burning flame of comprehension emerge from within the mind."[18]

For the Gnostic, education does not consist of learning about the world as God created it, the rebellious nature of man, the gracious work of God of redeeming fallen creation, or the wisdom of God as it has been given to man. The classical educational interests in matters of eternal truth, goodness, and beauty are "cages" put in place by people who are themselves confined to their ignorance. According to Weor, "It is absurd that adults—who are filled with prejudices, passions and antiquated preconceptions, etc.—run over the minds of children and youngsters when trying to mold their minds according to their rotten, dumb, and antiquated ideas."[19] Rather, Gnostic education is all about personal experience, and students should be encouraged to encounter for themselves, in their own way, what is most meaningful to them. To the Gnostic, this is more important and more trustworthy than any knowledge that has been received from the great thinkers of the past. Weor admonishes his readers: "We urgently need to demolish walls and break steel shackles in order to be free. We have to experience for ourselves everything that our school teachers and parents have told us as being good and useful."[20]

One can see these ideas all reflected in the writings of Montessori and Piaget: it is much better to let children learn what they want to learn, to set up an experiential classroom where, guided by their own divine wisdom, they will come to a realization of what is true, good, and beautiful for themselves.

Pink Floyd's iconic song, *The Wall*, can be viewed as an anthem for this type of education and a rejection of the classical methods of

Christian education. The message is that time-honored ways of teaching were just instruments that bludgeoned children into submission by teachers who mercilessly sought to limit students' free expression of their true selves. The song writer, Roger Waters, maintains that children who are taught facts and timeless wisdom are victims of thought control which permits them to think only things that have been approved by a blind and ignorant ruling class. With the intentional use of the double negative, Waters calls on students to rise up against teachers, and cast them and the classical education they provide into the dust heap. The rebellious children shout out:

> We don't need no education
> We don't need no thought control
> No dark sarcasm in the classroom
> Teachers leave them kids alone
> Hey! Teachers! Leave them kids alone.
> All in all it's just another brick in the wall
> All in all you're just another brick in the wall.

The song contains all the fundamental tenets of Gnostic pedagogy. Teachers are a hindrance to true learning. Structured, content-driven, classical education is all about thought control of which proper grammar is a chief weapon. Children should be free to learn what they want. Order and structure are agents of oppression. If children rise up against their teachers and cast them off, then they will experience authentic education.

Striking Where It Hurts

In the eighteenth and nineteenth centuries, two movements developed simultaneously in the church—Rationalism and Pietism. Rationalism elevated reason as the means to understand God and truth without the aid of supernatural revelation. For Rationalists, Scripture was a product of human impulses, and so it should be studied in the same way that the natural sciences were studied. By using empirical research and rationality, one could identify which aspects of Scripture did and did not belong to genuine Christianity. Pietism elevated inner spirituality as the means to discern a personal revelation of God's will. While the Pietists held that Scripture was the revelation of God, they placed a greater emphasis on the subjective revelation that came with studying Scripture. At first, the two seem unrelated. Rationalism appears to be anti-religious. Pietism appears to be intensely religious. Despite this, the two movements had much in common. Both:

- denied the importance of Scripture as the final revelation of God;
- rejected the doctrine of original sin;
- diminished the importance of the sacramental life of a Christian;
- believed that through educational reform they could create a utopian society; and
- maintained that confessional Christianity was a hindrance to the healthy development of the individual.[1]

Because of these similarities, it is sometimes difficult to tell who, among the leading educational reformers of the nineteenth century, was a Pietist and who was a Rationalist. For example, the famous educator Johann Pestalozzi (1746-1827) would at times write as an ardent Pietist. He promoted an intensely personal faith, warned against teaching children according to the catechisms of the church, and had close associations with leaders of the Pietist movement. At other times, he had all the marks of a Rationalist. He called for the restructuring of society according to Enlightenment ideals and praised the work of Rousseau whose book, *Emile*, was kept by his bedside throughout his life. Because of this blurring of Pietism and Rationalism, Pestalozzi was claimed by both camps as one of their own and his ideas were freely incorporated into their respective pedagogies.

The relationship between Rationalism and Pietism is useful in understanding the relationship between Gnostic education and liberal education. Like Rationalism and Pietism, one might assume that these are two different, unrelated positions. Gnosticism's chief interest appears to be exclusively spiritual. It is deeply mystical and outwardly deals with theological questions. Liberal education on the other hand exhibits little interest in the spiritual and appears to be rationalistic with many of its ideas coming from the anti-Christian, humanistic tradition of Marxism. However, both of these movements draw from the same intellectual well and share many of the same positions. They both reject:

- the possibility of a truth through revelation;
- the doctrine of original sin;
- the idea that authorities have been established by God and all doctrine (except their own) as a limitation on the individual; and
- the belief that children should be indoctrinated into Christ.

Because of these commonalities, Gnostic ideals can often be confused with more secular theories like that of liberal education. As a result, in colleges of education, the theories of Gnostics like Piaget and Montessori can be taught alongside those of Marxists such as Dewey and Vygotsky without any reference to their theological convictions.

The silence of the educational establishment on such theological positions does not make them go away. They are the fundamental doctrinal positions that underpin the theories, practices, and materials promoted by the American educational establishment. Each of these doctrines represents a direct challenge to the Christian confession and is at odds with the goals and objectives of Christian education.

How should a Christian educator, pastor, or parent respond? It is not simply by critiquing the methods or materials. These are merely expressions of the doctrines. It is by going straight to the heart of the matter and making a clear confession of what they as Christians, teach, believe, and confess within the context of the classroom. It is then possible to examine the practices, methods, and materials to determine if they reinforce and support that confession or detract from and weaken it.

The Rejection of Truth Through Revelation

> "This is eternal life: that they may know you, the only true God, and the one you have sent—Jesus Christ."
>
> John 17:3

The thought that there is something greater than ourselves is not a sentiment that pervades contemporary education. In educational paradigms, at best, God and religion are regarded as a private, individual matter that has no importance or relevance to how or what one should be taught. At worst, God is regarded as a wicked and capricious god, and religion is responsible for much of the world's evils. This alone should alarm Christian educators. Socrates, in Plato's *Republic*, warned against giving heed to any teacher who taught that God was the author of evil or misery. He said that such a teaching should "not be said or sung or heard in verse or in prose by any one whether old or young in any well-ordered common-wealth. Such a fiction is suicidal, ruinous, impious."[2] In spite of such an ancient warning, these very beliefs permeate contemporary educational thought. Little consideration is given to the possibility of a good and kind God that exists apart from ourselves, and that this might have an impact on how to approach education. The very fact that the educational establishment insists that all educational theory and methodology be based on "evidence-based research" presumes that the only trustworthy knowledge is what is learned through empirical research. This is known as "scientism." For this reason, the only teaching theories considered valid are those that have been observed in a lab setting. It does not matter that the church, for example, may have 2000 years of educational experience, or that there is a wealth of direction provided by the ancients on how children should learn. There is no reason to even consider that there might be other ways of knowing such as through philosophy or revelation, and that the insight gained from this might be even more reliable than what is purported to be truth by the social scientist. Scientism claims that the only truth that can be learned must exist within the realm of human observation in a controlled setting. This is a religious system to which the educational establishment is deeply committed.[3] Given that human reason and senses are the ultimate arbiters of truth, the conclusion of this system is that there is indeed nothing greater than ourselves. This concept is unique to our times.[4]

For almost two millennia, the driving force behind Christian education has been that there is one who is greater than us. He is the author of all wisdom and truth, and he has revealed himself so that we might know him and his wisdom. If children are to learn truth and wisdom, then they must see themselves as part of God's creation (contra liberal education) and know that God desires their salvation so much that he sent his Son into this world to redeem it (contra Gnostic education).

In orthodox Christianity, the fullest revelation of truth and wisdom is found in Scripture. Both the Old and New Testaments reveal Christ Jesus, who is the truth and wisdom of God made flesh. The twentieth-century theologian, Hermann Sasse, quoted Luther saying, "The Holy Scripture is God's Word, written and, so to say, spelled out and pictured in alphabetic letters, just as Christ is the eternal Word of God veiled in humanity."[5] This union of the eternal Word to human words makes the Word of God the sacred revelation of the eternal Trinity. Thus, in Christ alone, the Holy Triune God becomes knowable and describable. One of the great gifts of the Christian faith is that the unknowable can be known and precisely explained by using human words. God, in his infinite wisdom, could have revealed himself to man in any number of ways, but he chose to use human words. They are the means by which God chooses to communicate with us. This endows words with a certain sacred quality and demands that we use them in God-pleasing ways. For this reason,

Christian education has traditionally placed a great deal of emphasis on mastering language with its correct use of words and the rules of grammar. When they are used wrongly, they dishonor God and lead both speaker and hearer away from truth. However, when they are used properly, then they allow both hearer and speaker to know and understand God and the world which He created. For this reason, St. Paul emphasizes the need for Christians to use words properly saying, "No foul language should come from your mouth, but only what is good for building up someone in need, so that it gives grace to those who hear" (Ephesians 4:29).

The truth of God is not restricted to the words of Scripture. Through the centuries, the church has recognized that truth, wherever it is found, comes from Christ. When it is found outside of Scriptures—in what was classically referred to as "the poets and philosophers"—it still is from Christ. The difference is that the truth revealed in Scripture leads to forgiveness, life, and salvation whereas the truth revealed in the world does not.[6] Aesop's Fables are examples of this principle. More than just amusing tales for children, the church has long recognized that the stories communicate valuable truths about virtues and morality. The fables are useful for teaching any number of scriptural truths. For this reason, Luther recommended their use, saying,

> Aesop contains the most delightful stories and descriptions. Moral teachings, if offered to young people, will contribute much to their edification. In short, next to the Bible, the writings of Cato and Aesop are in my opinion the best.[7]

Clearly, Luther did not consider that the truth revealed in Aesop would lead to salvation, but he did recognize that it could only have come from God. If all truth is from God, then it is only natural that the more we learn of the truth taught by the poets and philosophers, the more we will appreciate the truth of Christ that is plainly revealed in Scripture. And the more we appreciate Scripture, the better able we will be to discern the truth that is revealed in the poets and philosophers.

One of Luther's great insights was that God, who reveals himself in Scripture, also hides himself in the world. As a result, when we look

...rld through Scripture, we see that God is intimately present ...ve. Sometimes we see a reflection of his power and majesty, ...isdom and beauty, but it is never a complete picture. From creation we cannot learn of the depth of sin, the incarnation of Christ, his death and resurrection, or the nature and work of the Holy Spirit. Those things are only found in the Word and Sacraments. Luther said,

> Although [God] is present in all creatures and I might find him in stone, in fire, in water, or even in a rope, for he certainly is there, yet he does not wish that I seek him there apart from the Word, and [thereby] cast myself into the fire or the water, or hang myself on the rope. He is present everywhere, but does not wish that you grope for him everywhere. Grope, rather, where the Word is, and there you will lay hold of him in the right way.[8]

How does this relate to education?

Sometimes people want to restrict Christian education to the parameters of "Bible learning." I once had a parent who would complain to me because the teachers in our school were not using exclusively "Christian" books and novels. He had the mistaken belief that truth and wisdom could only be found in the Bible and that secular literature was ungodly and should never be used in a Christian school. Others, and this is perhaps more common in contemporary schools, hold that "real" truth is found only in the world. Searching the Scriptures for truth is a matter of personal conviction and is best confined to church and Sunday school. Christian schools can unwittingly adopt this view by restricting theology to a religion class and a chapel service, and by adopting a curriculum similar to those of government-run schools which hold that theology has no bearing on pedagogy. Both positions are wrong. In Scripture we see the truth of Christ fully revealed; however, because God is hidden in the world, the truth found in the world is not unrelated, or unimportant. It aids in understanding and appreciating the truth revealed in Scripture, which, in turn, aids in understanding and appreciating the truth learned in the world. In both spheres, Christ is the source of this truth and wisdom. The Christian uses the former to serve the latter and the latter will always enlighten the former. This understanding also enables a joyful, even playful, approach to learning. It is almost like an academic game of "hide and go seek." As children seek out truth, goodness, and beauty, they discover the wisdom of God hiding in places they did not expect.

Johannes Kepler (1571-1630) is well known for his work in astronomy and his theories of planetary motion. One of his more engaging and entertaining works is a short essay entitled, "On the Six Cornered Snowflake," which he wrote as a New Year's present for his patron Matthäus Wacker von Wackenfels. In the essay, Kepler relates how one day, while crossing the Charles Bridge in Prague, a snowflake landed on his coat sleeve. As he looked at it, he wondered why every snowflake has six arms of perfectly symmetrical proportions. Why was this when there was no structural reason for it? He playfully explores various possible explanations, but each is unsatisfactory. There is simply no reason why such a temporary and fleeting object like a snowflake should have such a perfect design. The only possible answer is that the structure of the snowflake has no purpose– at least from a human perspective. It is simply a product of God's playfulness–a result of His creative work. It shows that He delights in the order of the smallest (and most fleeting) parts of creation.[9] It is an argument derived from the 1st Article of the Apostles' Creed. Kepler was able to arrive at this conclusion because he recognized the harmony between the truth in the world and the truth of Scripture. His conclusions about the beauty of the snowflake had to be in accord with the truth revealed in Scripture. Because truth cannot contradict itself, if what is learned in the world agrees with what is presented in Scripture, it is of Christ. If it contradicts Scripture, it is false and cannot be of Christ. Thus St. Augustine famously wrote,

> For we ought not to refuse to learn letters because they say that Mercury discovered them; nor because they have dedicated temples to Justice and Virtue, and prefer to worship in the form of stones things that ought to have their place in the heart, ought we on that account to forsake justice and virtue. Nay, but let every good and true Christian understand that wherever truth may be found, it belongs to his Master.[10]

Christians love true learning because it directs them away from false gods –especially from the god of self that cannot but lie and deceive–and towards the true God who created the world and everything in it.

The Rejection of Original Sin

> "For I am conscious of my rebellion, and my sin is always before me."
>
> Psalm 51:3

From the time of Jean Jacque Rousseau, a basic premise of the Enlightenment has been the denial of original sin. For the past three hundred years, Rationalists, Pietists, Gnostics, Mystics, Marxists, and Neo-Marxists have doggedly taught that children are born innocent and pure. But if this is true, why do they still act selfishly? The theorists would say that they must have learned this behavior from something or someone. So, who or what is to blame for this corruption? Pedagogues are not willing to blame their own self-centered approaches, so guilt is invariably placed on parents, churches, and communities. But, according to these enlightened "sages," all is not lost. If children have learned corruption from these institutions, it might be possible for them to unlearn it. Thus, contemporary pedagogues, with unending optimism, search for the latest methods of training children to reject these influences and act according to their supposed natural innocence.

In contemporary classrooms, this is manifested by what amounts to a pedagogical creed that insists that children should be praised and rewarded for everything that they do, and that the educator must avoid anything that causes hardship or suffering. American classrooms are to be incubators of self-esteem where children are flooded by a steady stream of positive affirmation. At times, this is taken to ridiculous extremes. Teachers are not to use red pens in marking tests because the color red is too threatening. Gym classes are not to employ games of elimination or even games that keep score for fear of damaging a child's self-esteem.[11] Teachers must use language that is affirming and inclusive so that students feel empowered. All of this grows out of the belief that, if we use the correct methods, children will cast off their bad behavior (at least whatever has been determined by the pedagogues to be bad) and achieve a corresponding level of righteousness. Rousseau, Pestalozzi, Froebel, Dewey, Piaget, Montessori, Vygotsky, and the many who have followed them have all claimed to have discovered the perfect way to accomplish this, but they have all utterly failed. Despite subjecting children to their prodigious research and innovative methods, they are still just as sinful, and society is just as corrupt as it was before the Enlightenment experiment began.[12]

"Indeed, I was guilty when I was born; I was sinful when my mother conceived me" (Psalm 51:5). The psalmist could not have put it more succinctly. Children are born sinful. A newborn can do very little on its own, but even before it can commit any sinful act, it was conceived as a deeply fallen sinner. A child's heart is so corrupt that, as it grows and develops more "autonomy"–the thing that liberal education prizes above all others–it will use that autonomy to sin. Children, like their parents, have hearts that are curved in upon themselves, and they will naturally seek themselves at the expense of their neighbor and the Law of God. Indeed, I have yet to meet a parent who had to teach his or her child to do something wrong. That ability is built right into them from the moment of their conception.

This is not to say that children are "bad." They may do naughty or sinful things but as a creation of God they have been endowed with the capacity to know good from evil, truth from falsehood, beauty from ugliness–in short, to know God Himself. However, because of the fall into sin, their nature is so corrupt that their desire will always be toward that which is contrary to God. It is true that children can be and should be taught to be kind, generous, respectful and the like. Theologians call this civic righteousness. But all the training in civic righteousness will never change the condition of the heart, and so it will always fail to address the root of the problem: sin.

Enter baptism. In this sacrament, the impossible becomes possible. Children, born anew through the sacred waters, are set apart to be "a chosen generation, a royal priesthood, a holy nation, His own special people" (1 Peter 2:9) and, as such, they are given a new life. In baptism, they have forgiveness and can look to God in faith with a renewed heart, choosing to use the good, the true, and the beautiful as they serve their neighbor in Christian love. This is not perfectionism. Even after their baptisms, children are still deeply fallen sinners who are capable of the most petulant sins, but they are also holy redeemed saints who can use the rich mercy of Christ for the good of others.

This spiritual dichotomy –the baptized as simultaneous sinner and saint –provides for a very realistic and sensible approach to education. Children, like adults, will always grapple with sin. At times they will be rude and selfish. They may be lazy, proud, boastful, and treat each other in some very mean ways. Some children may be better than others at covering up their sin, and some will excel at disguising their sin as righteousness. At such times, the educator will remember that they are all equally sinful and that there never has been, nor will there ever be, an educational theory that will be able to change that fact. Children will always be in need of rebuking, correction, discipline, and guidance. They must be taught the Law which will bring their sins to light and help them realize how they have failed in their vocation as student, son, or daughter. This is not to say that a teacher should never praise a child. Far from it. Children should be praised when they have accomplished something that is worthy of praise. That is a principle that educators throughout history have recognized; however, when praise is used to the point of denying a child's sinful nature, and when they are never confronted with the fact that they have failed in their vocation, then that is tantamount to a refusal to properly use the Law for its intended purpose. That is spiritually toxic to the child.

Schools should be places where children learn about the effects of the Law, but in measured ways. A comparison might be made with basic military training. Recruits are exposed to hardship: lack of sleep, the discipline of making beds, polishing boots, and the like. They learn how to lay still in the dark and cold for hours, and they practice mock battles in which they attack and are attacked. In modern military training, this is not done all at once, but incrementally so that soldiers gradually learn how to deal with these things in a controlled environment. The purpose is to give them the emotional and psychological tools to deal with hardships encountered on the battlefield. I am not suggesting that students should be treated as raw recruits in a boot camp with the teacher acting as a sergeant.[13] By no means. However, in the Christian classroom, students should learn about the nature of their own sin and be confronted with its consequences in a safe controlled environment. The purpose is not to put children down or belittle them. That would be contrary to their standing as redeemed saints of God. It is done to prepare them for a life lived under the cross: a life of repentance and forgiveness. When done properly, children will have the spiritual tools to deal with sin as it manifests itself in the heat of their own spiritual battles. As the Law convicts them of sin, they will be driven back to the forgiveness of Christ.

Often schools will advertise themselves with slogans like "We teach your child how to succeed." Perhaps a good advertising slogan for a Christian school would be "We teach your child how to fail." Granted, few parents would be enticed to enroll their children in such a school, but in reality, this is what Christian children need. Contemporary education with its endless rewards and positive affirmations causes children to believe that in life they should expect only success. The reality of life is that it is filled with failure and hardship, often stemming from our own sin. Confronting this failure is very difficult but crucial. Failure teaches us that we do not have limitless potential, but we are wholly and completely dependent on the mercy of a forgiving God. Children therefore need to be taught how to deal with failures and hardships and to understand them in terms of God's Law and Gospel.

The Rejection of Authorities Instituted By God

> "Let everyone submit to the governing authorities, since there is no authority except from God, and the authorities that exist are instituted by God."
>
> Romans 13:1

One of Luther's unique insights is the recognition that God has ordered society around three institutions or estates—the church, the family, and the government –as a means whereby He provides for His people and they, in turn, can serve their neighbor. These estates share three characteristics. First, they are divinely instituted and, as such, are ultimately accountable to God as the source of their authority. Second, each possesses a particular hierarchy or order designed to organize a Christian's life so that he or she can live securely under

God's providential care. Finally, each has a unique function that is necessary for the wellbeing of society. Each is a conduit for God's providential care for human beings–a channel by which He works for the good of all people.

It is no coincidence that modern educationalists, in their quest to perfect society, maintain that each of these estates needs to be swept aside and then recreated according to their utopian visions. This is a key driver of modern curricula and methodology. The fact that concepts such as "hierarchy," "order," and "authority" sound jarring to the modern ear is a testimony to the effectiveness of these efforts. In former times, these concepts were viewed in positive ways. They were seen as being necessary for a healthy functioning society. Now they have been successfully recast to be words of oppression and suffering—agents of many of society's ills. In light of this, the Christian educator must be especially vigilant. Children need to be taught the God-pleasing nature of these estates if they are to look to God in faith and to their neighbor with love.

The Estate of the Church

I used to teach an Introduction to Religion course to college freshmen. At the beginning of the semester, I would begin with the comment, "Throughout history, the church has done more harm than good: agree or disagree." Generally, between sixty to seventy percent of the class would agree with this statement—and this is at a Christian university. Most students were ignorant of the fact that, over the centuries, it was the church that fed the poor and widows; founded hospitals, schools and universities; and acted as a force for social good. These students, who had been thoroughly catechized in the philosophy of John Dewey and Lev Vygotsky, believed the church to be a human institution that controlled and oppressed the lives of millions of poor, ignorant people. It was essentially a corrupt institution that was responsible for much of the world's evil.[14] This is a telling example of how effective the prevailing educational philosophies have been at shaping the students' view of the world.

Christian children need to know otherwise. The church that Vygotsky and Dewey preached against simply does not exist. What does exist is the church of Christ. Scripture describes this church presented to God "in splendor, without spot or wrinkle or anything like that, but holy and blameless" (Eph. 5:27). It is holy and without blemish because it was divinely instituted, called into being by Christ. Within this church is the hierarchy of pastors and people. This is not a hierarchy of power, but one of mercy. Pastors have been entrusted with the task of shepherding and caring for the people of God. They are to speak words of absolution, preach divine mercy, and distribute forgiveness through the sacraments. The people look to their pastor, not in blind obedience, but trusting that the words he speaks are those of the Good Shepherd Himself. By this divine hierarchy, the unique function of this estate is fulfilled. Sinners are brought to the foot of the cross where they are liberated by Christ from sin, guilt, oppression of the evil one, and the curse of the grave. While it is true that evil people have committed sins in the name of the church, this does not negate its origins as a divine institution, its hierarchy, or its function.

The task of Christian educators is to teach students that the church is an estate that works good in the world. It is the only place where the forgiveness of sins may be found, and which bases its dealings with people on divine love and compassion. The most obvious way this is accomplished is in the worship life of the school, in particular the chapel service. Often school chapel services bear little resemblance to what the church does in the rest of her worship life. Often, they are reduced to simple, childish Bible songs with stories or chapel talks that are designed to amuse the children. But what does such a service communicate? Do the children view the church as a divine institution existing by the command of Christ? Do they see the pastor as a called and ordained undershepherd of Christ? Do they learn that the church is a sacred estate that exists for the forgiveness of sins? Or do they see the church from a secular perspective—an organization created by people that exists to keep them amused or devoted to making them feel better about themselves? Over two millennia, the church has developed liturgies and hymns that point to Christ and the forgiveness of sins, teach Scripture in all its beauty, and form a right understanding of the nature and purpose of the church. Given this, it is absurd that any Christian educator would want to strap on a guitar and teach children nothing but trite kiddie Bible songs or the latest in Christian pop music. It is much better to draw on the rich, ancient, and timeless liturgies and hymns to nurture in children a love for the "one Holy Christian and Apostolic church."

The Estate of the Government

The social evolutionists of the educational world would have us believe that we are progressing toward a better world in which all injustice and inequity will be eliminated. According to them, the agent for achieving this utopian world is the government. For this reason, government-run education is crucial as a resistance against the promotion of private Christian schools. Only in schools that have been guided by government-funded bureaucrats will children be properly indoctrinated so as to eliminate every evil: racism, sexism, genderism, sectarianism, and whatever else the enlightened believe to be a threat to progress. It is worth noting that there is something of a paradox here. Marxism holds that governments are inherently evil and are responsible for the oppression of the countless masses. So how can the government be the agent for good and, at the same time, the agent for oppression? For many, the solution is found in blaming the largely white male Christian leaders who have historically had far too much control. If their voice can be eliminated, or at least muted, then government can be reformed so it can work toward a society that has been perfected according to a set of predetermined ideals of equality and tolerance. Under such a government, all should have equal power and equal voice, except for those who are critical of the enlightened educational elites.[15]

This is not at all how Scripture depicts the world or the government. From the fall of Adam and Eve, sin has been the normative force that ensures the prevalence of injustice and inequity. To prevent this from devolving into chaos, God has instituted earthly governments. The hierarchy for this estate consists of rulers and the ruled. The rulers are God's representatives possessing their authority not from the people—as is so often claimed—but from God. The ruled, as part of their Christian vocation, are to render their rulers honor and respect, and to humbly and faithfully serve under them. The function of this estate is to enact and enforce laws to maintain order, provide for all people, and allow for the free proclamation of the Gospel by the church. Luther, in his *Sermon on Sending Children to School*, praised this estate, saying, worldly government is a glorious ordinance and splendid gift of God, who has instituted and established it and will have it maintained as something men cannot do without. If there were no worldly government, one man could not stand before another; each would necessarily devour the other, as irrational beasts devour one another.[16]

It is true that, at times, evil men use government in wicked and tyrannical ways, but that does not negate the estate. Even corrupt governments are institutions of God. Christian children need to see this and learn that part of their vocation is to be faithful citizens who do what they can to support good and honest government. This need is especially acute within the current climate of governmental dysfunction and societal breakdown. Christian schools need to be training children so they can take their place as virtuous leaders in government, business, and law, and exercise their vocation with Christian wisdom and humility. Luther went on to say,

> All these great works your son can do. He can become such a useful person if you will hold him to it and see him educated. And you can have a share in all this, and invest your money profitably. It ought to be a matter of great honor and satisfaction for you to see your son an angel in the empire and an apostle of the emperor, a cornerstone and bulwark of temporal peace on earth, knowing for a certainty that God so regards it and that it really is true. For although such works do not make men righteous before God or save them, nevertheless, it is a joy and comfort to know that these works please God so very much—and the more so when such a man is a believer and is in the kingdom of Christ, for he thereby thanks God for his benefits, bringing to him the finest thankoffering, the highest service.[17]

The Estate of Family

Much to the chagrin of those who believe that government-run education is the only acceptable way to raise children, Scripture contains no command such as "Governments, bring your children up in the training and admonition of the Lord." That duty rests with fathers within the estate of family. Like the estates of church and government, the estate of family is divinely instituted. Its origins can be traced back to the Garden of Eden where God bound Adam and Eve together as husband and wife and gave them the command to be fruitful and multiply (Gen 1:28). The hierarchy, in this case, consists of parents and children. Its function is to educate and nurture children in the wisdom of Christ. This estate operates under the 4th Commandment: "You shall honor your father and your mother" which, as Luther explained in the Small Catechism, meant that children should not despise or anger their parents but "honor them, serve and obey them, love and cherish them." Children are thus commanded to honor their parents because they have been placed there by God. By obeying this commandment, they also honor God.

The office of teacher, as an extension of the office of parent, falls under the 4th Commandment. Teachers function in the stead of parents, providing those aspects of the child's education that the parent cannot. Thus, when students honor, serve, obey, love, and cherish their teachers, they are doing a most God-pleasing thing.

With this in mind, it is a very poor idea to treat children as though they were parental peers, teacher associates, or the authorities who are responsible for what and how they should learn. And yet, this is just what prevailing pedagogical "best practices" call for. Children are taught to believe that they should not look to their teachers, but to themselves (Piaget) or to their peers (Vygotsky) for truth, goodness, and beauty. And so, teachers are to take the role of classroom facilitators or learning coaches. According to a popular educational catch phrase, teachers are not to be the "sage on the stage" but the "guide on the side."

If teachers are to be guides, who are the sages? According to modern pedagogy, it is the children. And so, children are encouraged to design their own curriculum, determine their own learning styles, and even establish their own class rules. One author recommends that students should draw up their own class constitution by which the teacher would promise to abide.[18] The message conveyed to children is that the 4th Commandment really does not apply to them, the estate of family is not important to their well-being, and they can, with impunity, rebel against the order instituted by God. Furthermore, it robs children of the opportunity to work out their vocation by faithfully serving those overseers whom God has given them—parents and teachers—and it unfairly burdens them with the office and responsibility that is not theirs to bear. Meanwhile, parents and teachers are absolved of their responsibilities under the excuse that, in so doing, they are "empowering children." Children don't need empowerment. They need training, guidance, direction, instruction, clear rules, and loving admonition. St. Paul said, "Honor your father and mother, which is the first commandment with a promise, so that it may go well with you and that you may have a long life in the land" (Eph. 6:2-3) So-called "enlightened" educational philosophers want children to disregard this commandment. But in doing so they also rob children of this promise.

The Rejection of Christian Catechesis

> "Speak the things that become sound doctrine"
>
> Titus 2:1

In 1517, Luther posted his famous 95 Theses on the Castle Church in Wittenberg. Nine of them began with the words, "Christians should be taught." These words quite literally launched the Reformation. In subsequent years, the Evangelicals established schools out of the conviction that Christ had commanded parents, pastors, and teachers to indoctrinate children. Central to the task of any Christian school, children are to be taught the gifts of forgiveness, life, and salvation. Proponents of modern education reject this. They contend that the clear and precise teaching of doctrine restricts a child's ability to think freely which results in an inauthentic faith. Indoctrination is taboo. Such claims are not just ridiculous, they are cruel. Suppose a person needed directions to get somewhere. No one would ever say to that person, "Your route must be authentic to you. Therefore, I won't tell you how to get to our destination. Instead, you must discover your own unique way;" essentially, "find your own way." Yet, this is just what much of contemporary pedagogy advocates; Children should always be allowed to discover truth for themselves in their own way, be affirmed in their understanding, and supported in whatever beliefs they might have formulated. Teachers are forbidden from providing clear teachings to children about how they should live or what they are to believe. Furthermore, a teacher should not correct a child who has a false belief or who is in error, else the teacher impose his or her own beliefs upon the child.

To claim that Christian indoctrination limits freedom, or that the teaching of it retards a person's ability to have a genuine faith, is not only a misunderstanding of the nature of faith, but also a rejection of Christ and the freedom that he alone offers from sin, death, and the devil. It is through that very doctrine that Christ accomplishes all those things. Luther said, "Life is fathered and fashioned by doctrine."[19] In other words, through the doctrine of forgiveness of sins, Christians are forgiven of their sins. Through the doctrine of Christ's resurrection, Christians are raised from death. Through the doctrine of Christ's victory, Christians are given victory over the devil. The more a Christian has been "indoctrinated" into the Christian faith, the more he or she can enjoy the fruits of that faith and be better defended by it against the enemies who seek to destroy faith. In reality, it is not the church that is guilty of limiting a child's autonomy, but those liberal educators who shrilly warn against the evils of indoctrination. By silencing all other voices—family, community, and church—they make it so that children are exposed to only one point of view—that which has been sanctioned by government-approved educators. However, for all their talk against indoctrination, their advocated philosophy is the very thing that prevents children from seriously considering anything else. One only has to ask teenagers about topics such as the role of government, personal liberty, nature of human sexuality, or end of life issues, and these supposedly autonomous people will almost always reply with what can properly be called "the party line."

Proper indoctrination into Christ leads to the most perfect autonomy possible. A fundamental truth of the Christian faith is that, without Christ, people are enslaved to the Law of God which demands obedience and threatens punishment. Efforts to achieve a righteousness working autonomously apart from Christ will always fall short of the Law's demands. The result is that instead of achieving true autonomy, the person ends up as an indentured slave to the Law. The answer for the modern educationalist is to cast off the Law which restricts people's free exercise of their autonomy, creates power struggles, induces guilt, and is responsible for many of society's ills. The problem with this approach is that they are blaming the wrong thing. The source of misery is not the Law of God, but the Law breaker. For true freedom from the Law, the Law breaker must turn in faith to the Law keeper: that is, Christ. He sets people free from the curses that come as a result of disobedience, and he gives a life of perfect freedom lived under his grace. The church calls this process of turning in repentance to Christ "catechesis."

Catechesis is radically different from what secular educationalists call "faith development." There are countless books and journal articles about how children understand faith, and how the Christian faith is to be developed in them. Authors talk about the development of faith in the same way one would talk about developing a roll of 35 mm film. If children have the right exposure to the right ideas in a proper learning environment, they will develop a genuine authentic faith.

In most Christian colleges, teachers generally take a methods class in which they learn to apply instructional strategies, based on developmental educational psychology, to the task of teaching the Holy Christian faith. As a result, most Christian schools have a "religion class" in which teaching faith is treated the same as every other subject. Teachers are instructed to use the same techniques, methods, and even assessment tools in teaching religion as they would for the teaching of spelling, math, or geography.[20] Faith development theorists have no problem with this because, by and large, they view faith as a universal, psychological phenomenon that can be classified in different stages of development.[21] Because they believe faith is rooted in the individual, they see nothing particularly unique about the Christian faith. Indeed, in many books that deal with the teaching of religion, you could scratch out any reference to Christ, substitute the name Mohammed, and it would make little difference.

Scripture is not so ambivalent. Far from being a psychological phenomenon, faith is described as quite an alien thing. In classical theology, faith is described in two ways: *fides quae creditur* ("the faith that is believed") and *fides qua creditur* ("the faith that believes"). *Fides quae* is the Christian faith that is taught by the church's creeds and confessions. It is the heritage of the church that is to be handed down from one generation to the next. As that faith is taught, the Holy Spirit, working through divinely appointed means, works *fides qua* in the individual which lays hold of Christ and clings to the *fides quae*.

It is true that this faith affects us psychologically and sociologically. In this respect, one can talk about having a "great faith," "weak faith," or "joyful faith," but these are only responses to the *fides qua* that has been implanted in the Christian. The Christian educator's task is not to make these responses the focus of catechesis, nor is it to create the ideal classroom environment where children will exhibit the proper response, whatever that may be. It is to catechize Christ's children so that they cling to the one saving faith (*fides quae*) in times of sadness, weakness, or joy.

The pattern for this molding process was not determined by a secular researcher, but by the Holy Christian Church. Secular research may be useful in explaining what the church does, or in gaining a different perspective on the work, but in the end, it is the church, which has 2,000 years of experience in catechizing Christians, that is best equipped to determine the substance and methods of this work.

In the Preface to the Large Catechism, Luther wrote about the nature of his own catechesis:

> But this I say for myself: I am also a doctor and a preacher, just as learned and experienced as all of them who are so high and mighty. Nevertheless, each morning, and whenever else I have time, I do as a child who is being taught the catechism and I read and recite word for word the Lord's Prayer, the Ten Commandments, the Creed, the Psalms, etc. I must still read and study the catechism daily, and yet I cannot master it as I wish, but must remain a child and pupil of the catechism—and I also do so gladly.[22]

Luther presented an image of himself as a child sitting at the foot of his teacher, eager and ready to learn. What does this Luther child/pupil need to learn? Clearly, he does not need to learn more information. Long ago he had memorized and mastered the simple words of the catechism and the Psalms. What the Luther child/pupil needed was to daily learn of his sin and God's grace. In praying or meditating on the words of Scripture, as contained in the catechism and the Psalms, Christ worked to give Luther what he needed the most. Through the Law, he was convicted of his sin, and through the Gospel, that sin was forgiven. This then is at the heart of Christian catechesis:

a meditation on God's Word that results in conviction through the Law and forgiveness through the Gospel.

In this way, catechesis is fundamentally different from education. Education is primarily involved with learning new information, the development of skills, and the nurturing of the intellect. Catechesis is about the formation of a Christian by Christ as he works through his means of grace. The monastic reformer, Bernard of Clairvaux (1090-1153), spoke of the need to approach the task of Christian formation differently than that of education.

> The instructions that I address to you, my brothers, will differ from those I should deliver to people in the world, at least the manner will be different. The preacher who desires to follow St. Paul's method of teaching will give them milk to drink rather than solid food, and will serve a more nourishing diet to those who are spiritually enlightened: "We teach, "he said, "not in the way that philosophy is taught, but in the way that the Spirit teaches us: we teach spiritual things spiritually." And again "We have a wisdom to offer those who have reached maturity."[23]

Traditionally, education focuses on conveying the proper knowledge. Catechesis is concerned with conveying Christian spirituality. It seeks to teach Christians to meditate on the holy things of God which were given to them in baptism: the Ten Commandments, the Creed, and the Lord's Prayer. Through such holy things, the Spirit works to teach the Christian spiritual truths. In the Ten Commandments, we learn what is required of us in order to properly serve God and our neighbor. We learn of our personal sin and how we have fallen short of the law. In the Creed, we learn of the good and gracious God who provides for all our needs, has sent his Son to redeem us from sin, and has given the Holy Spirit who brings us and keeps us in the one true faith. In the Lord's Prayer, we learn how to speak to this good and gracious God, asking for those things which are most needful in this life and the next. This encapsulates everything a Christian must know in order to properly meditate upon the entire Word of God, and to properly receive the gifts God gives through that Word.

While catechesis and education are different tasks, catechesis requires two things from education. First, it requires that catechumens will have been educated to know the nature of the words upon which they are to meditate. This means not just knowing the simple meaning of words but understanding and accepting the word of Scripture, not as a conveyor of religious sentiment or pious opinion, but as a conveyer of truth. Second, they must learn the skills and the patience to mull over what those words mean on a deep level. They must have a mind that will not pass over the words quickly, thinking that because they know the simple meaning, that they have understood everything. Instead, they must be disciplined to think carefully on the words and be willing to humbly spend time exploring them. In the Preface to the Large Catechism, Luther wrote,

> What else are these bored, presumptuous saints doing—people who will not read and study the catechism daily and have no desire to—except thinking that they are more learned than God himself and all his holy angels, prophets, apostles, and all Christians? God himself is not ashamed to teach it daily, for he knows of nothing better to teach, and he always keeps on teaching this one thing without proposing anything new or different.[24]

This does not discount the need for learning Bible narratives or a systematic instruction in doctrine. Christian children need to learn Bible stories because these narratives are the family history of the baptized. Bible stories provide the context for prayer by placing the baptized into the long history of God's dealings with His people. Doctrine teaches the baptized how to properly confess the faith that has been handed down to them. It equips children to speak precisely about their faith and defend it in the face of adversity. While both of these will be more educational in nature, a proper catechetical formation, with both the training in Scripture and doctrine, will prevent the teaching of religion to devolve into a mere intellectual exercise.[25]

The Effects

It is not uncommon for Christian educators and administrators to defend the prevailing educational theories as theologically neutral. "They are just methods that have little to do with theology," they will say. As hopeful as this may be, it is quite delusional. As one essayist put it,

> To ask whether religious education can learn from such figures may seem almost presumptuous. It is like asking whether Jack has anything to learn from a whole tribe of Giants, who treat him with a mixture of disdain and pity, and have every intention of finishing him off for dinner rather than giving him private tuition.[1]

In view of the philosophical and theological beliefs and motives of the people who proposed these theories, it is impossible to argue that there will be no negative effects. No one can claim that these theories are designed to support the goals of Christian education: to enable children to look to God in faith and their neighbor in love. In fact, they are designed to work against these goals quite successfully. As a result, a great deal of damage has been inflicted on individuals, the church, and society.

Harm to Individuals

The spiritual harm to individuals inflicted by these secular pedagogies should distress every Christian. It is nothing short of shocking to consider that, largely because of the education they have received, so many Americans have rejected the ancient Christian faith within the span of two generations. As children, they were recipients of faithful teaching by their pastors, teachers, and parents, and yet they abandoned those teachings as soon as they left home. The rates of apostasy are staggering. In a recent study of the Lutheran Church—Missouri Synod youth, roughly one-third were still attending church, one-third had left the church, and the whereabouts of the remaining one-third is either unknown or they are attending another denomination.[2] The retention rates of those who attended Lutheran schools are only marginally better.

Over the last thirty years, as the rates of apostasy were rising, the schools of the church endeavored to become more like government-run schools. Curricular standards set by the government were adopted, teachers were required to be certified by the state, and Lutheran colleges of education, responding to the demands of Lutheran school principals and education executives, transformed teacher training programs to mirror those in state-run colleges. As a result, students attending Lutheran elementary and high schools are taught in essentially the same way as their secular counterparts. They use the same curriculum taught with the same methods. It is true that there may be a religion class and a chapel service, but there is little else in the life of the school that is markedly different. If children have been educated with methods and materials that are designed to make them reject the faith, it should hardly be a surprise when they do just that.

This has not only happened in Lutheran schools, but also in Christian schools across America. Students have been taught in a way that makes it difficult for them to view the Law of God as an objective unalterable standard that all human righteousness fails to achieve. As the enormity of sin has shrunk, so also has the need for a Savior.

Not only has secular pedagogy hindered students' ability to grasp the nature of Christ's work, but they have also been robbed of the opportunity to see the unified wisdom of God as it is revealed in the world around them. In the modern Christian classroom, history has little to do with biology, literature has nothing to say to physics, and religion is taught in isolation, often using the same methods as all the other classes, with the addition of a 20-minute, once-a-week chapel service. This approach works against the message that there is one unified whole to creation: "one God and Father of all, who is above all and through all and in all" (Ephesians 4:6). As a result, students have difficulty seeing how God is woven through every part of their lives and everything that they learn. They can only look at God in isolation from everything else: good, perhaps, for a Sunday morning, but irrelevant to the rest of their lives.

Apple founder Steve Jobs was among the two-thirds who left the church. He grew up in a devoted Lutheran home and attended worship regularly with his parents at Trinity Lutheran Church in Palo Alto, California. According to Jobs, as a 13-year-old, he challenged his pastor on how God could allow children in Africa to starve to death. Supposedly the pastor replied that God's ways were beyond our understanding. Unsatisfied with an answer that placed God's mind above his, Jobs left the church vowing never to return. While he left the church, he did not leave religion. Instead, he fashioned his own religion incorporating elements of Zen Buddhism, Secular Humanism, and Epicureanism. While he believed this self-made religion was superior to Christianity, in reality, it was much harsher and crueler. It jettisoned mercy for self-improvement, grace for worldly success, and the promise of the resurrection for a life restricted to the here and now. Why would he reject a religion that is based on grace, kindness, and mercy in favor of one built on the self and material gain as a verification of righteousness? I believe that it was, at least partly, due to his educational formation. While I have no direct knowledge of Jobs' education, his approach to religion and theology represented everything that the educationalists of the twentieth century could hope for: a belief in his own inner divinity, the elevation of the authority of self, the rejection of authority, denial of a transcendent God, and a rejection of orthodox Christianity.[3]

Harm to the Church

Throughout her history, whenever the church faced theological challenges, she produced theologians who led her to a confession of the truth. When questions about the nature of Christ were under attack in the first centuries, Eusebius and Athanasius provided a clear confession of the truth. When challenged by Islamic intellectuals in Spain, Thomas Aquinas responded with an Aristotelian defense of Christian theology. When the doctrine of justification was being abused in the sixteenth century, Martin Luther produced the clear teaching of justification by grace through faith alone. These theologians were able to provide theological and intellectual leadership because their minds had been shaped by an educational model that enabled them to think clearly and creatively. Given the educational philosophies that currently dominate Christian education, is the church today capable of producing theologians with the academic and spiritual discipline required to respond to the modern threats it faces?[4]

The decline in church attendance in the West over the last half century was preceded by an equal decline in the theological rigor of the church as a result of numerous factors. Chief among them is the abandonment of the church's distinctive pedagogy. Instead of teaching children the way the great theologians of the past were taught, philosophies and methods have been adopted that have expressly been designed to stifle such development.

This neglect of Christian pedagogy has not just harmed the church at large. It has also had a deleterious effect on the local congregation. Healthy congregations require properly educated laity: people who know doctrine as confessed by the church and can incorporate it into the life of the parish. Such laity have become increasingly rare. As a parish pastor, I would often hear well-meaning parishioners at Sunday school teacher meetings, voter's assemblies, and Bible classes say things like, "All religions are the same," "We shouldn't judge others," or "All that matters is that you love Jesus." These comments came from people who had been catechized by faithful pastors. They had not learned those sentiments from the pulpit, or in Bible class, or in Confirmation Class, and yet they were so much a part of their personal piety that they could recite them as if they had been memorized from a catechism. At the same time, they had a great deal of difficulty speaking according to the confessions of the church. Even if they knew the correct doctrine, they struggled to enthusiastically support it. A key reason for this disconnect was that their minds had been so shaped by the pedagogies of Gnostics and Mystics, Marxists and Secular Liberals, that they were receptive to false, alien theologies and resistant to the orthodox theology. They couldn't speak the truth with confidence, were unsure of their confession, and were unable to help shape their own congregation as a confessing church.

Harm to Society

Throughout the long history of the church, schools have been the nurseries of some of the greatest artists, poets, architects, musicians, philosophers, and scientists. What these greats all had in common was that they received a classical liberal arts education. Bach could not have produced the music he did had it not been for his classical training in the liberal arts. His artistry was a product of his education in truth, goodness, and beauty, and his compositions were the result of his training in grammar, dialectics, and rhetoric. The same can be said of countless Christian intellectuals, scientists, and artists. Kepler and Mendel, Rembrandt and Caravaggio, Dante and C.S. Lewis were all shaped by a classical liberal arts education which enabled them to produce work that has been an enduring blessing to society.

Without detracting from contemporary Christian artists, authors, scientists, and intellectuals, consider how many young minds have been stunted by anti-Christian pedagogies. How many Buxtehudes or Tolkiens have failed to develop simply because they were not given the type of education that would encourage the flowering of their art? How many minds, ignorant about truth, goodness, and beauty, have been prevented from making godly contributions to society? It is impossible to quantify, but the effects of those losses are all too apparent. If politics has become simply a matter of name calling and stirring up opposition on the basis of raw emotion, perhaps it is because the church has failed to develop eloquent orators who can properly use emotion and intellect to move people to good. If popular music is little more than an incoherent production of noise overlaid with sexual energy, perhaps it is because the church has stopped producing musicians who write music that directs crushed sinners to the truth of Christ. If art has become a matter of offending the senses, perhaps it is in part because the church has stopped producing artists who can entice people to meditate upon godly beauty.

I am not arguing, as some do, that a renewal of classical education is the means of saving Western civilization. There are those who maintain that if the church can just produce enough wise and eloquent leaders for the government, the arts, and business, those institutions will reclaim a Christian ethos and a Christian way of thinking. Their perspective is that Christian classical education brought the light of

Christ to pagan lands in the past, and that same style of education will renew Christ's presence in the West—especially in America—today. However, it was not education that brought Christ to light for the Romans, Europeans, or Americans. It was the Gospel as it was preached and administered through the sacraments, the means by which Christ was revealed and people renewed. Society's renewal in the past was because people, having been enlightened by the Gospel, sought out Christ as he was hidden in the world. This impulse then led to a flowering of the arts and sciences. Meanwhile, the world has benefited from the Church's educational work as a result of the church's faithfulness to the Gospel. If the schools of the church employ secular pedagogies, this will not happen, and society will be poorer for it. However, if the church trains children according to her rich educational heritage—teaching children the nature of truth, goodness, and beauty as it is found in Christ—the world will be blessed because of it.

Part II

Applying the Antidote

The Cure Of Timeless Standards

Throughout this book I have made reference to truth, goodness, and beauty as central features of Christian education. Throughout the church's 2,000 years of educational history, they have been core features of her pedagogy. Dating as far back as the ancient Greeks, the most important aspect of education was learning about truth, goodness, and beauty. They were the standards that transcended time, location, and even culture. They provided the overarching framework for understanding the world and our place in it. What was true then is true now. What is beautiful is beautiful in every place. What is good is good for all people. Because they are universal and timeless, they were understood as the revelations of God's nature. According to the Greeks, God had woven evidence of these standards into every part of creation and had instilled in people a desire for truth, goodness, and beauty so that they would seek Him out. Though each had its own distinct property, they were so intertwined that they really could not be separated. For example, if you described truth, then you were also describing beauty and goodness. Over all of this stood God who was the ultimate, the overarching standard to which we are beholden.

Everything that was taught in ancient Greek schools fits under the framework of truth, goodness, and beauty. Natural philosophy, which included what we refer to as natural science, human nature, and some aspects of theology, was concerned with truth. Art and architecture, which centered on aesthetics, was concerned with beauty. Theology, with its study of ethics, was concerned with goodness. And all education was to direct students to the divine unity of all things.

The First Standard: Goodness

The ancient understanding of goodness was much deeper than what our post-modern mind allows for. Good in our contemporary culture is a matter of opinion. It is occasionally argued that if a majority of people agree that something is good, then it must be. For example, often moral matters such as the marriage of homosexual people will be judged as good because opinion polls indicate that most people believe it to be so. For the ancients, this was a disastrous way of understanding good. Plato, with his famous cave allegory, wanted people to break free of society's assumptions of what is good and grasp the ultimate good (God). This was the ultimate standard for which all people were to strive. While it was impossible for human beings to achieve this, it was possible for people to grasp the good things which came from God such as virtue, ethics, and the meaning of life—things that might be called moral goodness.

There are many ways to define good; however, for the purposes of this brief discussion, it is sufficient to use Aristotle's definition of good as the measurement of how perfectly a thing fulfills the purpose for which it was created.[1] For example, a lawn mower is good if it cuts the lawn evenly and quickly because it does the job for which it was designed.[2] A discussion of what makes for a good lawn mower might be easy, but what about those questions that deal with moral goodness, virtue, and ethics? For example, what constitutes a good life or good government? What makes for good children, husbands, or wives? What is a good job or a good use of money? These are much more difficult questions that every Christian will, at some point in his or her life, have to face. Asking students to work as a group to come up with answers to those questions, as is so often done in contemporary classrooms, is foolish. If they do not know the purpose for which those things were created, they will arrive at the wrong conclusions. To correctly answer such questions like that requires an education in goodness.

When I was in college, I thought that Baby Duck was a good wine. It was a Canadian, low-alcohol bubbly wine that was overpoweringly sweet and fruity. It was basically effervescent, alcoholic, grape juice. At the time, I thought it was everything a wine should be, but that was only because I did not know much about wine. I did not know anything about acidity, tannins, naturally occurring sugar content, or the different grape varietals. I had to be taught about those things and only then could I distinguish between good and bad wine, with Baby Duck firmly belonging to the latter category. That principle applies to the need for students to be taught goodness. Contrary to Maria Montessori, who maintained that children would naturally know what is good, we cannot let them determine good for themselves. Not only will their sinful nature tilt them away from good and toward evil, but they have very limited knowledge of what constitutes good, and unless they are very lucky, they will probably get it wrong.

Christian educators cannot afford such a gamble because they are dealing with matters that are a great deal more important than cheap wine. They are training children for vocations in which they will have to make determinations of good on a daily basis. Students must be trained to ponder questions like "Am I fulfilling the purpose for which I was created? What about the person whom I am to marry, my children, my job, what I spend my money on, the candidate that I am to vote for, the people I choose to call friends, how I use my time?" These all involve determination of good and require students to know why they were created. But our educational system leaves children wholly unprepared for this task, opting for useless pithy phrases like "whatever they choose is good just so long as it is authentic to them."

The Second Standard: Beauty

"Beauty is in the eye of the beholder" is regarded by many as a philosophical absolute. Anytime there is a disagreement over art, architecture, clothing, hairstyle, tattoos, or body piercings, it is not too long before someone solemnly utters the phrase and effectively silences all debate. The phrase asserts that no one can, with any certainty, judge something to be ugly or unsightly. Those who do so are narrow-minded and intolerant. Some will wrongly attribute this pearl of wisdom to Plato—a belief that only strengthens its power to silence, for who can argue with Plato? Not only did Plato not say this, but he would have emphatically denied it. He maintained that there is a perfect beauty, apart from ourselves, and this beauty has its origins with God. In reality, few, if any, really believe beauty is completely subjective. If you were to go for a relaxing stroll on a beach and come upon a rotting, decomposing fish, you would not claim that it was beautiful. Similarly, I have yet to meet the person who averts their eyes from a sunset claiming that it is simply too hideous to look at. So despite the popularity of this philosophical maxim, there are broadly accepted standards of beauty.

The phrase "beauty is in the eye of the beholder" appears to have its origins in the book *Molly Brawn* by the nineteenth-century romantic novelist Margaret Wolfe Hungerford. I suspect that the phrase became widespread because it captured the philosophies of the nineteenth and twentieth centuries which maintained that only empirical knowledge was reliable and valuable. Because beauty could not be analyzed or measured in a laboratory, it had to be subjective. If beauty was relative, how could it be taught in school? So, like goodness, educationalists abandoned the task of teaching beauty and turned their backs on a tradition dating back to the ancient Greeks, if not earlier. Aristotle held that beauty was expressed in "order and symmetry and definiteness" and had a special connection to the mathematical sciences.[3]

For Plato, beauty was eternal and moved humans to seek after harmony. Though they could never have a perfect understanding of beauty, it was a window to the spiritual and the divine. By studying beauty, students could know more about God. They would also learn how to use beauty for the good of society and the betterment of the state.

St. Augustine taught that God wove beauty into every part of creation. He wrote, "Every creature has a special beauty proper to its nature, and when a man ponders the matter well, these creatures are a cause of intense admiration and enthusiastic praise of their all-powerful Maker."[4] God created man with the ability to appreciate beauty so that he would not love the base things of the world but would look to God. A rigorous education in beauty refined students' understanding of what God was like and enabled them to recognize his presence in the world.

The medieval theologians linked beauty to meditation and worship. Using the criteria of proportion and light, they deliberately incorporated these into their sacred art and architecture. Proportion was a divine mathematical harmony of structure and a manifestation of the order of God. Light, the essence of color, was required for visibility and was understood as coming from God who was the source of all light. The great cathedrals of this period were shaped by the desire to connect worship with divine beauty. These places of sacred meditation had perfect proportions and were flooded with the light of intricately designed stained-glass windows. Beauty was anything but something found in the eye of the beholder. It was a confession of who God was and how he was manifested in the world.

With the rise of the pragmatism of Dewey's Progressive education in the twentieth century, one of the central dogmas of education was that every part of the curriculum had to be practical. Consequently, the study of beauty, or aesthetics, began to recede. At first, subjects like physics, chemistry, biology, and geography were given preferential status. Later on, in an effort to become ever more practical, school curricula became saturated with "useful" subjects such as finance, civics, nutrition, and, more recently, social media management and stress management. This movement has ensured that the teaching of beauty was completely pushed out of the curriculum. Few teachers are aware that aesthetics was ever an academic discipline.

The belief that beauty is subjective has effectively expelled all timeless standards from the classroom. If beauty is relative and if truth, goodness, and beauty are so intertwined that they can be used almost interchangeably, then it only stands to reason that truth and goodness are also relative– they too must lie in the eye of the beholder. Furthermore, if truth, goodness, and beauty are descriptors of God, then God must also be relative. He can only be what I make of him or how I perceive him, not who he objectively declares himself to be. If all of this is true, then why teach anything of truth, goodness, and beauty—indeed anything of God—in the modern classroom? It is far better to stick to those "practical" subjects like social media awareness and stress management. At least then students won't feel too anxious as they scroll through their newsfeeds!

The Third Standard: Truth

With Jesus standing before him, Pilate asked "What is truth?" As a Roman student, Pilate would have read Cicero, Virgil, Plato, and Aristotle all of whom talked at length about the nature of truth.[5] He would have also learned about the Roman mythological figure Veritas (Truth) who was the daughter of Chronos (Time) and the mother of Virtus (Strength), the goddess of bravery and military virtue. Veritas was held in such high regard that every Roman citizen was obliged to offer her worship. Truth was so important to the Romans that it was integral to the honor code of the military. Pilate would have been taught that unchanging truth had been bequeathed to the Romans from ancient times. It was at the root of everything that a Roman considered to be noble and worth fighting for. At the same time, Pilate knew that the Roman Empire was by no means the ideal state envisioned by Plato: one that was governed by truth and virtue. As a politician, he had to reconcile the ideals he learned as a student with the reality that, in life, truth was often compromised for the sake of political expediency. In this context, the bloodied and beaten Jesus proclaimed himself to be a different type of politician: a king in whom all truth was made manifest. To Pilate, Jesus said, "You say that I'm a king. I was born for this, and I have come into the world for this: to testify to the truth. Everyone who is of the truth listens to my voice" (John 18:37). In the kingdom of Jesus, all the ideals that Pilate had learned as a student from the philosophers and mythology were a reality. Here was a spiritual kingdom in which truth was never subverted for the sake of expediency, but molded strangers and foreigners into sons and daughters of the King of Truth. The citizens of this kingdom spoke truth, meditated on truth, even ate and drank truth. For a Roman, like Pilate, this probably seemed so fantastic that it was too good to be true.

The ultimate reality is one who is truth incarnate, Christ Jesus. Jesus does not claim to provide access to the truth like some divine guru, nor does he claim to simply teach truth to his followers. His bold claim is that he is truth made flesh. This incarnation of truth is so potent that it conforms people to his image. Here then is truth that loves his people and in turn makes them into lovers of the truth. As Paul wrote, "Those he foreknew he also predestined to be conformed

THE CURE OF TIMELESS STANDARDS

to the image of his Son" (Romans 8:29). The people who are conformed know the truth of who they are, why they are, and what they are to do.

This is not at all how the modern secular pedagogues understand truth. They do not see eternal truth as one of the great standards that students must strive after. They believe truth is restricted to something functional that is determined by empirical science. From this perspective, if we can discover how things are put together, what they are made of, or the process by which things happen, then we will know the totality of truth. In a strange way, it is remarkably close to Aquinas' definition of truth as conformity of the intellect to reality as determined by God, except the god is science.

While the information discovered by scientists may be factually and functionally true, science cannot be the source of transcendent truth because it is not the true and living God. Pope Benedict XVI wrote:

> The functional truth about man has been discovered. But the truth about man himself—who he is, where he comes from, what he should do, what is right, what is wrong—this unfortunately cannot be read in the same way. Hand in hand with growing knowledge of functional truth there seems to be an increasing blindness toward "truth" itself—toward the question of our real identity and purpose.[6]

Truth is not just a matter of what is true—such as the boiling temperature of water—it is a matter of the deep questions with which everyone grapples. "Who is God?" "Who am I?" "What am I to do with my life?" "What is going to become of me after this life is over?" Those are all questions that only Truth (Christ Jesus) can answer. The answers he provides give meaning, purpose, and direction to the functional truth of science because they show how it can be used for the good of one's neighbor.

The Standard That Binds It All Together: Unity

The unity of the three standards, or measurements, is perhaps the hardest to define, and yet it is crucial for the proper understanding of the nature of the curriculum in a Christian school.

The ancient Greeks looked at the universe as a unified whole designed to draw one closer to God. By understanding the interconnectedness of all things, a person could begin to grasp the things of God. Medieval Christian teachers continued in this tradition. Truth, goodness, and beauty were worth learning because they were expressions of the oneness of God. Goodness described what God was like, but so did beauty and truth. There wasn't a multiplicity of truths or goods or beauties any more than there was a multiplicity of gods. While they are distinct, the three were intertwined. Truth interpreted beauty and goodness, goodness gave insight into truth and beauty, and beauty informed truth and goodness. Each described one aspect of the whole. It was similar to the way the Athanasian Creed describes the Trinity: "Such as the Father is, such is the Son, and such is the Holy Spirit." While there are three persons of the Trinity, each distinct and unique, yet there are not "three gods but one." Similarly, truth, goodness, and beauty added something unique to a person's understanding of the world while being part of the same unity. So no matter what "subject" students studied, they were learning about the same thing from different perspectives.[7]

In schools today, the very opposite approach holds sway. Subjects are compartmentalized with teachers (particularly in the upper grades) restricted to teaching subjects for which they have state endorsement. Each "subject" is taught in isolation with little regard for how they are interconnected. What does biology have to do with music, or what does art have to do with math, and what do any of the subjects have to do with theology? The modern pedagogue would reply, "Very little." In contrast, virtually every educator from Plato to the beginning of the twentieth century would have replied, "Everything." They all understood that each "subject" was in some way connected to God, the source of all wisdom, and should relate to truth, goodness, and beauty. This is also the position of Scripture. Paul talked about how all wisdom points to Christ. In Ephesians he said,

> This grace was given to me—the least of all the saints—to proclaim to the Gentiles the incalculable riches of Christ, and to shed light for all about the administration of the mystery hidden for ages in God who created all things. This is so that God's multi-faceted wisdom may now

be made known through the church to the rulers and authorities in the heavens (Ephesians 3:8-10).

The term "multi-faceted" (πολυποίκιλος), can also be translated as the "multi-colored wisdom of God" highlighting the kaleidoscope-like quality of God's wisdom that is revealed through truth, goodness, and beauty.[8]

This sense of unity should permeate every aspect of Christian education. In the confessions of the Evangelical Lutheran Church, it is understood that there is only one doctrine—that of Christ—which is expressed in different ways. While it is possible to talk about the doctrine of Baptism, the Lord's Supper, Justification, or Sanctification separately, are all understood in the context of the one doctrine of Christ. David Scaer has likened Christian doctrine to the various ingredients of a cake that are all mixed together to form one batter.[9] Similarly all subjects are avenues to a further understanding of the one truth, goodness, and beauty which is of the one God. Unity demands that theology and pedagogy join hands as a unified whole to shape the curriculum, methodology, content, catechetical practices, and prayer life of the school.

Using the Standards the Wrong Way

Over the long history of the liberal arts, one philosopher has exerted a continuing influence: Plato. The contribution he made to the Western understanding of the liberal arts is hard to overstate, but certain elements of his educational philosophy were contrary to sound Christian doctrine.

Plato believed that all human beings had a divine ability that enabled them to use truth, goodness, and beauty to lead themselves to the divine. To him, godliness was a human work, an achievement of the maximum human potential. The conundrum that Plato faced was this: how could one know for sure that something was in fact true, good, or beautiful? Emotions were too fickle: too easily misled by the base passions of the world. One could "feel" that something was good or true or beautiful, but those feelings were not trustworthy. So how could one be sure? The answer lay in the intellect. Aided by philosophy, Plato regarded the intellect as a sure and trustworthy guide. And so, it became the task of education to teach children to subordinate their emotions to their mind so that they could properly use truth, goodness, and beauty in their quest for the divine. Consider a modern-day character for illustration. Mr. Spock, from the original *Star Trek* series, represented the Platonic ideal: mastering logic, subordinating emotions, and using intellect as a way to access the sacred. The fictitious Vulcan maxim, "The needs of the many outweigh the needs of the few" harkens back to Plato's *Republic* in which Socrates argues that philosophers, who were guided by pure reason, were best positioned to be leaders of the state because they would be concerned about the good of the whole community and not be guided by selfish interests. From a Christian perspective, there are two things wrong with Plato's understanding. First and most problematic is that he elevated the ability of man to find God. Plato did not acknowledge the doctrine of original sin, and so he had no problem with the idea that man could approach God using his own powers. The second problem is that he elevated intellect over emotion, believing that emotion could always mislead, while intellect was always reliable. Plato did not share the scriptural perspective that, while both intellect and emotion are gifts of God, they are also equally corrupted by sin and are only reliable when they are made subject to the rule of faith. As the church incorporated the liberal arts into her pedagogy, she also imported Plato's optimistic view of man as well as his view of the trustworthiness of the intellect. The great Dutch educator, Desiderius Erasmus (1466-1536), was influenced by this Platonic ideal. He believed that the liberal arts opened the eyes of students to truth, goodness, and beauty, and made them more truthful, good, and beautiful. This was as much a renewal of the spirit as it was of the intellect. Erasmus believed that if a purified form of the classical liberal arts were introduced in schools, godly, virtuous citizens would be produced who would reform both the church and society according to Platonic ideals. In some ways it was not unlike the goals of the Enlightenment philosophers who came two centuries later. They also believed that education was the way to a perfect society.

    The renewed interest in the classical liberal arts that has happened over the past twenty years has been refreshing indeed. With its academic and theological rigor, a new vitality has been breathed into the church's task of educating her children. However, with the recovery of this ancient model of education, there has also been a resurgence of Platonic thought. Some will speak of the classical liberal arts as introducing children to Christ (Plato's "divine"). Using language that is reminiscent of Montessori's "divine embryo" talk, some will speak of children possessing a divine spark or having an element of God's consciousness. For example, a widely accepted research center, the CiRCE Institute, states that "Classical educators have a high view of humanity. To the Greeks, mankind possessed a divine spark. To the Christian and Jew, he is the Divine Image."[10] This divine spark enables students to use the eternal standards to find God and become virtuous people. Some classical education advocates maintain that their pedagogical approach will lead to a renewed Christian society. As virtuous students take positions of leadership in business, law, and politics, there will be a renewal of faith and a rebuilding of a Christian society. As a result, classical liberal arts is viewed as a means for rebuilding a ruined Western civilization and recapturing America's place as "a city on the hill."

Occasionally, Philippians 4:8-9, "Whatever is true, whatever is honorable, whatever is just...," is used to buttress the argument that the liberal arts form a path to spiritual and civic renewal. If we do our part, learning the true, good, and beautiful, then God will do his part and bless us with his renewing presence (..."and the God of peace will be with you"). This is problematic because no one can ever perfectly attain such a goal. Consequently, no one can be completely assured of the peace of God. No matter what sort of education we have received, our desire is to think and practice the opposite of what is true, good, and beautiful. Paul's words from Romans 7:18-19 put an end to the Platonic ideal of spiritual renewal through education, "For the desire to do what is good is with me, but there is no ability to do it. For I do not do the good that I want to do, but I practice the evil that I do not want to do."

Because of the dangers of such ideals, the confessions of the Evangelical Lutheran Church speak forcefully against any effort to endow the human spirit with the potential for spiritual renewal. The *Formula of Concord* states,

> [We reject] that in the human being, human nature and its essence are not completely corrupted but that people still have something good about them, even in spiritual matters, such as the capability, aptitude, ability, or capacity to initiate or effect something in spiritual matters or to cooperate in such actions.[11]

And further on:

> We believe, teach, and confess that the unregenerated human will is not only turned away from God but has also become God's enemy, that it has only the desire and will to do evil and whatever is opposed to God.[12]

If we allow for some Platonic spark of the divine or claim that God can be found solely through the philosophers and poets, be they ancient or modern, we contradict these confessions and end up aligned with the likes of Rousseau, Dewey, Piaget, Vygotsky, Montessori, and all the proponents of liberal education who claimed that people are born righteous: that we all have the inner ability to do good works. It is only a matter of degrees. The Liberals, Gnostics, and Mystics claim that students are wholly righteous, and the Neo-Platonists claim that students have a spark of righteousness, but both make education a spiritual work with the responsibility for renewal resting with the student.

While it is natural for man to desire truth, goodness, and beauty, the sinful nature will always abuse those things. It will always try to appropriate them as its own and use them for self-aggrandizement and self-justification. For example, we may desire truth but will seek it in the opinions of those who agree with us, instead of in Christ. We may desire goodness but will look to issues such as environmentalism or social justice to prove we should be counted as good.[13] We may desire beauty, but will use cosmetics, fashion trends, or body sculpting to achieve a fleeting external beauty so that others will admire us. Such self-appropriated truth, goodness, and beauty distorts our perspective so that we end up becoming the opposite of what we desire. Our truth becomes a lie, our goodness becomes wickedness, and our beauty becomes ugliness.

While our sinful human nature seeks to impress God with self-appropriated claims on the transcendent standards of truth, goodness, and beauty, they are of no worth to him. *Theologia Germanica*, a medieval devotional text prized by Martin Luther, spoke of this:

> Man fancies himself to be what he is not. He fancies himself to be God, yet he is only nature, a created being. From within that illusion he begins to claim for himself the traits that are the marks of God. He does not claim only what is God's insofar as God becomes man or dwells in a divinized person. No, he claims what is the innermost of God, God's prime mark, namely the uncreated, eternal Being.[14]

Any attempt to make these standards our own, defined by us, or originating in us is an assault on the 1st Commandment because it pushes God out of His role as the sole source of truth, goodness, and beauty, and destroys the unity that is found in Him alone. Mark Mattes puts it this way,

> Thus they do not think they need God's generosity or mercy, but instead believe they are entitled to God's grace. Luther will have none of that and ends up distinguishing a creation beauty from a gospel beauty. Beauties in creation do not exist for securing one's status *coram deo*. They do not serve as stepping-stones on which one can jump on the way to establishing eternal life.[15]

Truth, goodness, and beauty are not rungs of a ladder that we can clamor up in order to get closer to God, nor are they instruments by which we can save society from the effects of sin. In the Heidelberg Disputation, Luther says, "The man who thinks that he wants to attain grace by doing his best (*faciendo quod est in se*) adds sin to sin, so that he becomes doubly guilty."[16] When properly used, truth, goodness, and beauty do not make us into better people. Instead, they reveal what sinful and unrighteous people we are. Properly used, they function as Law, and the more a person travels down the Platonic road, the deeper the Law cuts. It may cut when a person realizes that the pursuit of the truth, goodness, and beauty has been motivated by sinful pride. In this case, he or she may try to create something true, good, or beautiful, and become quickly filled with pride over what has been achieved. The presence of such pride instantly defiles truth, goodness, and beauty because that creation is no longer pure. The cutting of the Law is also experienced when a person is brought to the realization that perfect truth, goodness, and beauty is forever beyond reach. I believe that theologians, philosophers, artists, writers, musicians, and the like, are particularly susceptible to this thinking. When they honestly apply themselves to their craft, they quickly realize that, though they have done their very best, they still fall short of what they know to be the ideal. Listeners may hear an outstanding performance by a musician and may even think it to be the most beautiful thing that they had ever heard, but the musician knows the flaws of the performance. In this way, the law of beauty accuses the musician that, despite his or her best efforts, perfection is unattainable.

Perhaps it is because of the accusatory nature of the Law that many educators have given up on teaching truth, goodness, and beauty. If it is impossible to attain these eternal standards, why even try? It is better to settle for "the eye of the beholder" approach and allow students to do whatever pleases them. This is not an option for the Christian educator. The Law of God is good even though it condemns (Romans 7:12), and so also truth, goodness, and beauty are good even though they condemn. They are good because they come from God. The Christian teacher therefore will use the law of truth, goodness, and beauty to teach children to turn from seeking to use their own ability to achieve righteousness and look instead to the truth, goodness, and beauty that is in Christ.

In Christ, there is a radically different paradigm of these eternal standards. Christ turns them on their heads. Though he was perfect truth, he took on man's deceitfulness so that man might abide in the truth. Though he was perfectly good, he took on man's wickedness so that his Father in heaven might call man good. Though he was the most beautiful of all, he took on all of man's ugliness so that man would be called the beloved in the Lord. And all of this deceitfulness/truth, wickedness/goodness, and ugliness/beauty is most fully displayed on the cross.

In the Heidelberg Disputation, Luther said, "But he is worthy to be called a theologian who understands the revealed things and 'backside' of God (*posteriori Dei*) [Exodus 33:23] as being seen through sufferings and the cross."[17] From the philosopher's perspective, the cross of Christ is the very opposite of truth, goodness, and beauty;

but when viewed from Scripture, it is the very source of those things. Paul said in Corinthians,

> God's foolishness is wiser than human wisdom, and God's weakness is stronger than human strength… Instead, God has chosen what is foolish in the world to shame the wise, and God has chosen what is weak in the world to shame the strong. God has chosen what is insignificant and despised in the world—what is viewed as nothing—to bring to nothing what is viewed as something (1 Cor. 1:25, 27-28).

Christ does not just teach about the truth, goodness, and beauty, nor does he simply lead his people to them. Through baptismal indwelling, he remakes people so that they radiate a new cruciform version of truth, goodness, and beauty in their everyday lives. On account of Christ's work, Christians are made into true people, good people, beautiful people, who rejoice as they find those things in the world around them, recognize them as gifts from Christ, and use them to praise God and serve their neighbor. The cruciform transcendent standards are found in the most unexpected places: the bedside of the sick, the care of the helpless, the teaching of the young, and so on. They may take the form of a well swept floor, an honest count of change, or a carefully plowed field. The world may regard these things as unimportant, lowly, or even ugly, but the Christian sees them as places where God, though masked, is present with his truth, goodness, and beauty.

Such an understanding reveals the world to be an enchanted place filled with wonder and mystery. The natural and the supernatural are a unified whole in which the Triune God permeates everything and where the truth, goodness, and beauty of Christ show where we least expect them.[18] Luther captured this sense of richness,

> Whenever you listen to a nightingale, therefore, you are listening to an excellent preacher. He exhorts you with this Gospel, not with mere simple words but with a living deed and an example. He sings all night and practically screams his lungs out. He is happier in the woods than cooped up in a cage, where he has to be taken care of constantly and where he rarely gets along very well or even stays alive. It is as if he were saying "I prefer to be in the Lord's kitchen. He has made heaven and earth," and He himself is the cook and the host.[19]

Luther saw the beauty of Christ in the nightingale who, with its simple song, offered praise to God and directed Christians to the Gospel. This is the world that classical education sets before a child: not an unattainable ideal, but one in which the student already lives. Through the teaching of the transcendentals, Christian educators seek to broaden the horizon of their students so that, as they discover the world around them, they can discern the many and varied manifestations of God's truth, goodness, and beauty. This world is refreshing and radically different from anything that Plato ever imagined.

Treatment Protocols

Content and Methods

In the sixteenth century, Desiderius Erasmus talked about the importance of using engaging methods to teach young children. Among the more innovative methods he suggested was to make letters out of paper, stick them to a target, and have students spell out words by shooting arrows at the letters.[1] I like to bring up that example when educators insist that teachers were ignorant about student engagement in the past and that today, because of modern research, we are so much better at it. While I am sure that a good number of educational professionals would recoil in horror at the thought of students handling weapons, Erasmus demonstrates that good teachers have always recognized the value of what is now called "active learning." A cursory reading of the great educators of the past reveals that they recognized the importance of making learning pleasurable and warned against teachers who were unconcerned about engaging students. While they were interested in good methods, this was only secondary to good content.

Historically, content drove education. Content-driven education sought to provide students with the building blocks of knowledge to use as the basis for all future learning. This pedagogical premise, which was the standard in Western education through to the middle of the twentieth century, is now dismissed as hopelessly outdated. The argument is often advanced that, because students have such easy access to the internet, there is no reason for a teacher to concentrate on content. Therefore, it is better to use the time teaching children to be "life-long learners" and let them look up what they need to know on Google.

There are two problems with this approach. First, it makes a child's learning dependent on the results that Google provides. Could it be that Google, like many of the tech firms of Silicon Valley, manipulates their results to match ideological positions of race, gender, and religion? Douglas Murray, in *The Madness of Crowds*, points out the biases that are embedded in search engines such as Google.[2] A search on "straight white couples" yields a page in which there are only four images of actual straight white couples in the first four lines with the rest being of homosexuals and interracial couples. A search done for "European Art" includes seven images of people of color in art and eleven images of women in the first fifteen images. It includes an imitation of the famous Da Vinci "Creation of Man" in which both God and Adam are portrayed as black women. A student searching for these things might well assume that straight white couples were anomalies and that a majority of European art dealt with women and blacks. The other problem with the "Let them Google it" approach is that children can't search Google for something they don't know exists. For example, if a student is unaware that America was involved in World War I—and yes, I have had college students who were unaware—they will not search for the reasons America entered that war. Furthermore, information that they do happen to find will be without context or meaning. Far from expanding a student's understanding of the world, this approach stunts it. If they have only been given engaging activities in their classroom and left to construct their own understanding of the real world, they will forever be unaware of the world of ideas that exists beyond their limited horizon.

I used to try to have a discussion with my education students about the influence of neo-Marxism in modern education. It was generally a futile exercise because, not only were they ignorant of the basic tenets of Marxism, they couldn't even identify who Karl Marx was. They lacked the content required to critically examine how this ideology influenced their methods and curriculum. As a result, they became unwitting accomplices in the promotion of neo-Marxist ideals which were directly contrary to their confession of faith. These were generally good students, but they were products of an education system that placed maximum value on methods and minimal value on content.[3]

A content-driven curriculum is especially important to Christian education because it concerns itself with teaching enduring knowledge that students will use for the rest of their lives. In doing so, it implicitly communicates that there are timeless standards, and that students live in a world of big ideas and monumental events that are important apart from their personal perspective. This is a vital lesson to learn considering that the Christian church seeks to catechize students into a faith that lays claims to the biggest ideas and the most monumental events of all time. This lesson is only learned through understanding the content of those ideas and events.

The starting point for content-driven education is rote learning or memorization.[4] One of the popular education myths is that rote learning is a hindrance to creativity and critical thinking. Conveniently ignoring the fact that almost all the greatest creative minds throughout history did copious amounts of memorization as students, opponents will claim that rote learning should rarely, if ever, be employed. It is telling that one method that is almost never taught in colleges of education is how to teach memorization. However, as any parent who has read the same story over and over again can attest, it is how young children learn. They thrive on it. Since the time of the ancient Hebrews, rote learning at a young age has been understood as an essential component for developing creativity because it provides students with a storehouse of information. As they mature, they can then draw on this storehouse to make connections with seemingly unconnected bits of content to synthesize something new.[5]

In the beginning stage of a classical liberal arts education rote learning occupies a substantial portion of the curriculum. This gradually decreases as students mature and teachers introduce other methods such as deductive reasoning. It is much like learning to play the piano. No student masters the piano simply through a "meaningful encounter" with music. Mastery requires the rote learning of notes, sharps, flats, and proper fingering. There are countless hours of scales, drills, and repetitive exercises. Beginning students will learn to play a few simple tunes, but rote learning is the primary means of instruction. Once the drills have been mastered, students gradually progress to the point where they are able to interpret music, and from there, they learn to assemble notes in completely new sequences to compose music.

That same pattern applies to almost all learning. Parents naturally use rote learning to teach their children to speak. Through repetition and parroting, children learn vocabulary, grammar, spelling, syntax, and the uncountable nuances required for the effective use of language. This continues until the children can use that language to learn on their own by reading and engaging in intelligent discourse. Finally, they combine all the knowledge they have acquired to creatively formulate new ideas. And so, the journey to creativity started with memorization.

Rote learning is not only the key to creativity, but also essential for proper catechetical formation. Augustine understood that the ability to meditate on the transcendent things of God was contingent on a person's ability to memorize. Without memorization, there was nothing to meditate on. Luther held that memorization was a sacred gift. The ability to memorize was a mark of man's spiritual nature. Irrational creatures could see, hear, and feel; but it was the spiritual man who could remember and meditate.[6] He likened rote learning to a cow digesting its food. As a cow regurgitates its cud in order to extract more nutrients from it, Christians recall or regurgitate the Word of God they learned as a child to mull over and extract new insights and understandings. It all begins with rote learning: children memorizing the Ten Commandments, the Apostles' Creed, the Lord's Prayer, psalms, hymns, and spiritual songs. As they do so they acquire a sacred language that the Holy Spirit uses to work faith and understanding. These words are in turn used to offer praise to God and edify their neighbor.

The Curriculum of the Christian School

Teachers live in a world of kids with colds, forgotten homework, and a love of recess over reading. Because of this, they tend to be very practically minded people. Unlike university professors who delight in musing over the most esoteric of topics, teachers want direct instructions as to how to get things done. The nature of their profession leads them straight to the heart of the matter: "How do

I teach this or that subject?" To all the teachers reading this, I'm afraid that I am going to disappoint you because I am not going to provide a detailed prescription for what should be taught in a classical Christian school. There are many other sources for this. More importantly, though, there is simply no "one size fits all" model of classical education. What is appropriate for a school in a rural northern Ontario town may not be suitable for a Texas suburb. What works in a farming community in Iowa may not work in New York City. Teachers, as the master learners, are the best equipped to structure the curriculum and select the materials appropriate to the situation. However, it is worth examining a few areas of the curriculum in order to illustrate how theology shapes both content and methods. While I do this from a distinctly confessional Lutheran perspective, Christian teachers from other confessions may find it useful to examine the impact that their own confession of faith has on particular subjects. For the sake of brevity, I will look at language, music, science, and history.

Language

Toward the end of the 2019 movie, *Tolkien*, J.R.R. Tolkien, who has survived the horrors of WWI, has a conversation with his priest, Father Francis. Tolkien asks the priest what he has been doing. Father Francis replies, "I spend every afternoon with mothers, with widows. What can I say to them? 'Your sons have died in a war to end all wars.' Words are useless—modern words anyway. I speak the liturgy. There is comfort, I think, in distance, in ancient things."[7] As Father Francis pointed out, the best language is found in ancient words—the words of the liturgy. For this reason, language occupies a prominent position in the classical Christian curriculum. Christ, the eternal Word of God made flesh, is not only the master of all words but, by his act of redemption, has given his words to his people to be used for holy purposes.

This has a two-fold importance. First, words are the means by which Christ works in the life of his people. Luther saw that the imperative of the 3rd Commandment (Remember the Sabbath Day by keeping it holy) was to "keep that Word holy and gladly hear and learn it."[8] Because God enters the lives of His people through the

Word, the intent of the command is that, as God's people occupy themselves with meditating on His holy Word, they are sanctified. Luther wrote, "Truly, we Christians ought to make every day such a holy day and devote ourselves only to holy things, that is to occupy ourselves daily with God's Word and carry it in our hearts and on our lips."[9] Such meditation is important because words possess formative power in that they produce what they describe. Through the words of Scripture, God creates and sustains faith; and so, when God speaks words of truth, goodness, and beauty, those things are created in the lives of his people.

Second, Christ, as the master of words, has redeemed words to become holy objects that are used in service to one's neighbor. In the explanation of the 8th Commandment, "You shall not bear false witness against your neighbor," the Small Catechism states that we are to choose our words so that we "defend him [our neighbor], speak well of him, and explain everything in the kindest possible way." Christians need to know the best words to use in the best ways so that they may be of benefit to others. This twin emphasis should have a profound impact on what is taught in the Christian classroom.

In government-run education, literacy training receives a great deal of attention and money—so much so that a whole industry has developed around it. Unfortunately, for all the billions of dollars spent, there seems to be little to show for it. In 2016, up to forty percent of those who completed the ACT writing exam failed to demonstrate the skills required to pass the most basic university level English class.[10] Obviously, there are many contributing factors; however, one cannot ignore the way language is viewed within the educational establishment. One might assume that literacy would include the appreciation of literature as an art, challenging students to understand the fullness of literature. Unfortunately, this is not so. One of the great criticisms of the now famous Common Core curriculum is that it all but ignores literary forms such as poetry, fiction, and short stories. Literacy in modern educational parlance stands for something much different and represents an altogether different understanding of language than is traditionally assumed.

Colleges of education across America promote a Neo-Marxist view of language which holds that words are tools used by dominant groups to oppress the minorities. Accordingly, insisting that children use words "properly" perpetuates "classist" power structures put in place by the oppressors (which are invariably described as white, male, and Christian). Apparently, it is better to let students assign their own values to words and encourage them to use language in a way that is authentic to them. Given this, why should students be concerned about things like incomplete sentences or subject-verb agreement? They have learned that it is better by far to express their thoughts in their own ways. Often, I have had college students who will write something that is factually wrong, illogical, or just grammatically incorrect, and when confronted they will say, "That's not what I meant." In their minds, the words they use aren't as important as what they meant, and it is my job as a professor to interpret their words in order to find out what they are really trying to say.

While Christian educators want their students to be able to read and write correctly, they should have a much higher goal. They should seek to instill in their students a reverence and respect for words. This begins with a careful and deliberate instruction in grammar, spelling, and penmanship. From the moment children pick up their pencils, the message should be conveyed that they are dealing with something special and they need to form their words properly. This need has become increasingly acute as many teachers have themselves never learned the basic rules of grammar, let alone how to teach it. A *New York Times* article revealed that fewer than half of 3rd through 8th grade teachers had taken a course in university taught on how to teach grammar and writing.[11] Building this respect for words also involves selecting the highest quality literature—both in prose and poetry.

Much of what is currently promoted as good children's literature is judged primarily on its social message. The world of children's literature is awash with stories that preach (and I use that word intentionally) gender inclusiveness, globalism, environmental activism, feminism, and self-centeredness under the guise of self-esteem. Obviously, Christian educators will want to choose literature that is congruent with a Christian worldview, but their first concern should be that it is well written and of enduring quality.

Perhaps the best way to convey respect and reverence for language to students is through teaching the sacred languages of the church—Latin, Greek, and Hebrew. There are many excellent arguments for teaching these languages, but three are especially pertinent.[12]

First, if students only know one language, they are confined to that language and are unable to view it objectively. A student who knows Latin, Greek, or Hebrew can examine their native language with greater objectivity. The sacred languages provide a perspective on English grammar and vocabulary that allows students to choose their words with care and precision. While the same can be said for learning any foreign language, the sacred languages provide a unique perspective in that they are the languages from which English developed. Personally, it was through learning Greek that I began to truly understand English grammar: an experience common to many beginning Greek students.

Second, learning a sacred language enables students to study Scripture and the church fathers in their original tongue. It allows them to "listen in" to Moses, Isaiah, Luke, and Paul speaking in their own language. They can eavesdrop on Jerome, Augustine, Luther and Johann Gerhard as they discuss the theology of the church. Reading the original languages can be likened to being brought into a great lecture hall that is filled with the greatest churchmen and theologians of all time, listening in on the conversation without the aid of a translator.

Third, the sacred languages are the church's defense against false doctrine. Humanly speaking, the Reformation of the sixteenth century would not have happened had it not been for a revival of the sacred languages in the fifteenth century which drove many young theologians, such as Martin Luther, to read the Scriptures in their original languages. In so doing, they were able to peel away the layers of false doctrine that had built up over the centuries to reveal the true doctrine of Christ. Luther wrote,

> For the devil smelt a rat and perceived that if the languages were revived, there would be a hole knocked in his kingdom which he might have difficulty stopping....They are like an unwelcome guest who has come to his house; so he determines to show him such entertainment that he will not tarry long. Very few of us, my dear sirs, see through this wicked plot of the devil.[13]

We live in an era when the very foundations of language are under assault. For the modern pedagogue, words do not convey truth: all that counts is personal interpretation. It is a most effective angle of attack; because if words do not convey truth, then all Christian doctrine must fall. If the neo-Marxists view language as a means of oppression, then the language of the church—her confessions, her doctrine and even her liturgy—can be dismissed as ancient tools for controlling minds. For the church to survive as the confessing Bride of Christ, she must go on the offensive and teach her children the languages of Scripture.

If contemporary educational experts say that words are mere constructs subject to whatever value the individual places on them, then the church must teach children language as a way to communicate objective truth. If the pedagogues of government-run schools say that the ancient languages have no place in a modern classroom, then the church must vigorously teach those languages to her children. This is not to say that every schoolteacher or homeschool parent will be able to teach Latin, Greek, and Hebrew. Practically speaking, few are capable of the task; however, that should not stop educators from introducing students to sacred languages. It is possible for any teacher or parent to begin with teaching basic Latin and, if there are the resources and abilities, to move to Greek and even Hebrew. Even if students never master those languages—as most won't—they will have grown in their appreciation and respect for those enduring words as the tools by which God communicates truth to them.

Music

For most people today, music is valued simply as a form of entertainment. Few consider its educational value as a vehicle for conveying something deeper and more meaningful. While people have always enjoyed a good tune, for the greater part of educational history, music had a much more significant role. The ancient Greeks appreciated performed music, but within academic circles it was treated primarily as one of the sciences. It was a mathematical study of the harmony of sounds in time. This perspective can be traced back to the philosopher Pythagoras (570-490 BC) who noted that the planets moved together in mathematical symmetry to produce an inaudible harmony of music.

This mathematical understanding of music made its way into early Christian pedagogy. When people like St. Augustine sought to "Christianize" the liberal arts in the fifth century, he retained this Pythagorean understanding of music, adapting it to support Christian theology. Augustine believed that the educational value of music was in its representation of the mathematical order and perfection of God.

This understanding more or less continued to dominate Christian education until the Reformation when Luther turned the study of music on its head. While he still appreciated the mathematical aspects of music, he saw the chief purpose of music as moving the soul to contemplate on the grace of Christ and give thanks to God.[14] The role that Luther and the Evangelicals assigned to music in the school curriculum was arguably one of their more significant contributions to education. Luther could never speak too highly of music, calling it "an outstanding gift of God" and valuing it "next to theology."[15] Music was of such importance to Evangelical pedagogy that Luther believed it to be an essential prerequisite for every teacher. He said, "He who knows music has a good nature. Necessity demands that music be kept in the schools. A schoolmaster must know how to sing; otherwise I do not look at him."[16] Music was seen by Luther as a "semi-disciplinarian" and a "school-master" moving students to be "more gentle and tender-hearted, more modest and discreet."[17] Much more than a mere liturgical ornamentation or an object of aesthetic beauty, music was valued for its rhetorical qualities as it moved a person toward the good and away from evil and demonic influences. These beneficial effects came not just by listening to music but by participating in it, and so every student was taught to sing, mostly in the songs of the church.

When confessional Lutheran schools were established in America in the nineteenth century, the attention given to musical instruction was virtually unmatched by any other public or parochial school system of the time. Every Lutheran school teacher was so well trained that often he served as the parish musician. The church body published carefully planned music curricula for all age levels and prescribed singing for the first hours of the school day. Music was valued as an indispensable tool for teaching the doctrines of the Evangelical confession and communicating an understanding of personal Christian piety. The very best music that they had for accomplishing this was the Lutheran chorale.[18] In Lutheran schools, children were taught a standard set of chorales which were also sung by the congregation. A commonly used curriculum was the *Liederpensum* which, if followed, resulted in children memorizing 156 stanzas of 36 hymns and chorales by the end of 8th grade. This regimen would equip children to sing by heart around the family table and join in congregational singing during the Sunday morning Divine Service.[19]

As Dewey's model of Progressive education became fashionable in the twentieth century, the nature of music education changed. Music became valued for its therapeutic effect, role in building cultural literacy, promotion of self-expression, and development of creativity. This influence was felt in Lutheran schools as music appreciation gradually replaced the singing of chorales. While singing was retained, often children were taught "age appropriate" Bible songs that educational experts had deemed to be more meaningful to children.

This shift brought with it a decline in musical literacy. Until the mid-twentieth century it was natural for people to sing together at home, in schools, and, of course, in churches. Today, communal singing in general has become a foreign activity and rarely will people hear the songs of the church outside its walls. Music has become simply something that is performed—a commodity to be consumed and measured for its entertainment value. According to some reports, less than fifty percent of the population is able to read the most basic of music, and few Christians have a hymn repertoire that extends much beyond *Amazing Grace* and *How Great Thou Art*. Lost is the tool that Evangelical educators used to teach doctrine and build piety: the chorale. For a church that depends so heavily upon congregational song, this presents a crisis. In a liturgical church, congregational singing constitutes up to fifty percent of the service. If people cannot sing, their ability to participate in congregational worship is limited, and they are prevented from experiencing the full catechetical force of the hymns and liturgy. It is little wonder that, in many churches, music has been reduced to a "contemporary Christian" band that "performs" for the congregation, leading them in simple, easy-to-learn, pithy refrains.

Evangelical children must be taught their own rich musical heritage and hymns by giving the music of the church its proper place in the Evangelical curriculum. It does not require a lot of technology, expensive curricula, or highly specialized training. All that is needed are a few good hymnals and the most inexpensive and universal of all instruments: the human voice. If educators dare to travel down this well-marked path of musical education, their students will be well prepared to join with the "angels, archangels and all the company of heaven" in offering up their voices in full-throated songs of praise.

The Sciences

The liberal arts have been historically divided between the lower and higher arts. The lower three arts—Grammar, Dialectics, and Rhetoric—belonged to the Trivium which constituted the building blocks of all future learning and equipped students to read well, think cogently, and speak eloquently. The four higher arts—or the Quadrivium—were numerical arts. Arithmetic (numbers in sequence), Geometry (numbers in space), Music (numbers in time), and Astronomy (numbers in space and time) equipped students to understand the world around them. In the medieval period, these higher arts, or sciences, enabled students to see the world as an intricately ordered creation of God and prepared them to study theology. Science prepared a student to understand theology, and theology gave a proper understanding of science. For this reason, theology was deemed the "Queen of the Sciences"—the ultimate goal of all learning which Luther called "the head of all branches of knowledge."[20] Few today would give theology that title.[21]

Those who struggle to see how the liberal arts relate to science are positively stumped when it comes to the relationship between theology and science. To contemporary minds, science is a practical subject that deals with the "real world," and theology is subjective, unprovable, and irrelevant for daily life. They contend that theology has little to say to the modern human condition and less to say to the current reigning monarch of the educational world—science. However, science is in greater need of theology today than at any time since it started its ascent. Why? Because science is searching for answers that only theology can provide. I would further posit that Evangelical theology is best equipped to provide these answers because it gives a unique value to that which concerns the modern sciences—the physical world.

The misnamed "Enlightenment" of the eighteenth century separated theology from science.[22] Philosophers contended that the physical world was the sphere of the secular and theology the sphere of the spiritual. Because of this separation, theology was excluded from any discussion about the physical world. The church, all too willingly, went along with this. However, the truth of Christ's work of redemption reveals that there is no such thing as a truly secular world. In Christ, everything is sacred. Christ became flesh and blood to redeem both body and soul, effectively making the physical and the spiritual realms sacred. This is what Paul refers to when he says that Christ is "in all, through all, and over all" (Eph. 4:6). Christ is hidden in the physical world which means that, while He cannot be seen through a microscope or a highly advanced algorithm, He is revealed through the Christological lens of truth, goodness, and beauty. Without that lens, there is only human observation which, because of humanity's fallen nature, is faulty and liable to misinterpretation.

In speaking about the importance of science in education, President Barack Obama said, "[Science] is more than a school subject, or the periodic table, or the properties of waves. It is an approach to the world, a critical way to understand and explore and engage with the world, and then have the capacity to change that world..."[23] He reflected a commonly held view that science is capable of providing the answers to the really important questions in life. The problem is that science only provides information. It cannot furnish the wisdom required to properly interpret and apply what has been learned. Christ's truth, goodness, and beauty allow us to use the knowledge gained through science rightly, employing it for the good of our neighbor. With the advancements in scientific research, the need for this perspective is paramount. The progress of technology has highlighted the need for a strong understanding of ethics (goodness). For example, the development of genetic manipulation of human embryos requires an understanding of the 1st Article of the Creed. Similarly, social media sites, with their capacity to destroy a person's reputation on a whim, require that programmers possess an understanding of the 8th Commandment. If the programmer or scientist does not have a grounding in goodness, what will inform his or her decisions? Now, more than ever, we need leaders in science and technology who understand the transcendent standards and can incorporate them into technology for the benefit of mankind.

Instead of segregating theology from science, classical Evangelical education brings the two together and treats them as part of the unified whole of education with Christ illuminating both. Science is the domain of Christ every bit as much as is theology. This does not mean that science should be taught as a Bible-based subject, or that every assertion has to be proved from Scripture. Not only is that an artificial construct and a poor application of Scripture, but there is simply no need for it. The physical world is already a sacred place in which God works by his providential care to supply the needs of mankind. A truly enlightened approach—enlightened by the Christological understanding of truth, goodness, and beauty—will reveal that.

Not only does theology enlighten science, but the reverse is true as well. Natural science is an indispensable tool for understanding the fullness of God. This led Luther to write,

> With the support of the mathematical disciplines—which no one can deny were divinely revealed—the human being, in his mind, soars high above the earth; and leaving behind those things that are on the earth, he concerns himself with heavenly things and explores them. Cows, pigs, and other beasts do not do this; it is man alone who does it. Therefore man is a creature created to inhabit the celestial regions and to live an eternal life when, after a while, he has left the earth. For this is the meaning of the fact that he can not only speak and form judgements (things which belong to dialectics and rhetoric) but also learns all the sciences thoroughly.[24]

From this Evangelical perspective, science becomes a journey of discovery that reveals the world to be an enchanted place filled with wonder and mystery, where the natural and supernatural come together to produce a vastly more complex and intricate world than anything that the secular scientist could ever imagine. When a modern astrophysicist studies the stars, all he sees are faraway gaseous bodies. His discipline will only allow him to postulate about their composition, their age, the effects of their existence, and so on. When Johannes Kepler studied the stars, he pondered those things as well, but he also saw a revelation of God's providential plan made evident through the patterns of the cosmos.[25] He wrote, "Certainly such is the divine handiwork of the Good and Great God...the immense world is sacred."[26] To Kepler, the natural world was a book to be read not in opposition to, but alongside, Holy Scripture. Both have the same author, and both reveal the same God. When compared with the way science is taught in government-run schools, where it is presented as a set of unrelated facts devoid of meaning, this classical Evangelical perspective is enticing indeed. Not only does it engage students with the meaning of what is learned, but it also allows the church to reclaim her rightful role as a teacher of both theology and science.

History

The introduction to a commonly used high school history textbook contains the following explanation of the study of history:

> We adopted two themes that serve as the spinal cord of our history: "technology and the environment" and "diversity and dominance." The first theme represents the commonplace material bases of all human societies at all times. It grants no special favor to any cultural group....The second theme expresses the reality that every human society has constructed or inherited structures of domination.
>
> Thus when narrating the history of empires, we describe a range of human experiences within and beyond the imperial frontiers without assuming that imperial institutions are a more suitable topic for discussion than the economic and social organization of pastoral nomads or the lives of peasant women.[27]

The book maintains that history is about how various power groups (usually almost exclusively defined as white, European, and male) have subjugated various weaker groups and constructed a historical narrative that perpetuates their power structure. It views the historian as one who identifies dominant oppressive narratives and gives voice to the oppressed. This view is not restricted to this particular textbook. The prevailing approach in American education today is that history teaches no grand themes, enduring truths, or unifying lessons. It is simply a disparate assembly of personal narratives reflecting different perspectives. It does not matter whether the narrative is of an illiterate peasant or a leader of a great kingdom. Each has his or her own personal perspective of equal value. Furthermore, according to this approach, history is not the unfolding of events as a result of actions taken by people, but as the random result of economic, social, or political trends and structures. For example, it would claim that the Reformation did not happen because Luther took a stand based on his theological convictions, but because the social conditions of Germany were such that the oppressive structures put in place by Rome had to be overthrown. In the summer of 2020, the New York City Department of Education committed itself to dismantling institutional racism and reversing its effects—without defining what institutional racism is—and to teaching students "stories of people of different races, abilities, genders, ethnicities, languages, and more" so that they learn to value difference and diversity.[28] This is just one example. Across the nation, it is a safe bet that state boards of education will become more adamant about building curricula around diversity, inclusion, and identity politics and there will be many who insist that this imperative be extended to Christian schools.

The church has her own approach to history that has proven itself to be supportive of the confessions of the church and beneficial for her people. It is first of all theocentric: it is about God arranging the affairs of men for the execution of His will. Far from being a series of disconnected events, there is an overarching narrative, a rich and intricate tapestry, with each thread revealing God's providential care for his creation and the working out of His plan of salvation. In *To the Councilmen in All Cities in Germany,* Luther wrote that "they [chronicles and histories] are a wonderful help in understanding and guiding the course of events, and especially for observing the marvelous works of God."[29]

The Evangelicals of the sixteenth century saw history as a portal that allowed students to step into the world of the past and learn from the examples of both the wicked and the godly, the evil and the virtuous. Writing about the value of history, Luther said that children learned how "God maintains, governs, hinders, advances, punishes and honors men, according as each one has deserved good or evil." As history chronicled moments of divine action, it was incumbent upon the teacher to relate historical accounts "as if they stood in Scripture." For this reason, historians were to write histories "with extreme care, fidelity and truth."[30] In the Evangelical schools of the sixteenth century, children were to be taught history "not only in Holy Scripture, but also in heathen books, how men introduced and held up the examples, words and works of their ancestors." This was especially important for those who would someday become civic leaders. Luther urged, "Therefore, it would be of the greatest value to the ruling class if from their youth up they were to read, or have read to them, history books, both sacred and secular. They would find in these books more by way of example about the art of ruling than in all the law books."[31]

What can the modern Evangelical educator learn from this? First, we must cast a critical eye on modern approaches to history. Like all other aspects of pedagogy, the way one approaches the study of history is not neutral. The Christian teacher cannot simply incorporate state-recommended approaches without weakening the Christian confession. A curriculum that cannot acknowledge the God who directs history or will not identify either wicked or virtuous historical figures, will be working against the aims of Christian education.

Second, we need to develop a modern theocentric understanding of history. We cannot replicate how history was read in the sixteenth century, nor should we want to do so. We live five centuries away from that time period. But can we not develop a history curriculum that centers on God's grace in Christ Jesus, the Lord God as the God of history, and how he orders the affairs of men for good? Such a curriculum should not romanticize the past. It should accurately depict people with their weakness and sin exactly the way Scripture describes them. Not only would this be in accord with what we teach, believe, and confess, but it would be an infinitely more edifying view of history than anything that is currently promoted by our secular pedagogues.

Third, history needs to be integrated into the broader curriculum. It is not a stand-alone subject. The study of science is incomplete without a knowledge of the history of science. The study of literature is diminished if not placed within its historical context. Theological controversies occurred in the context of historical events. History needs to be understood as part of the unified whole in which every aspect of the curriculum is part of the overarching recounting of the story of God working in the lives of men and shaping the affairs of the church.

A Classical Liberal Arts Education: The Training of Christian Thinkers

Over the past two decades, there has been a growing interest in classical liberal arts education among conservative Christian educators that has transcended confessional boundaries and has found receptive ground among the Lutherans, Reformed, Orthodox, and Roman Catholics. Classical Christian liberal arts education now represents the fastest growing segment of the Christian educational "marketplace." While many traditional parochial schools have been closing, classical Christian schools have been opening up, often without any assistance from parent church bodies. This grassroots movement is driven by parents, pastors, schools, and parishes searching for a pedagogy that is authentic and faithful to the church's confession. Many teachers have been drawn to it because they are tired of the revolving door of education theories. They also recognize that the prevailing pedagogies of American education are hostile to the Christian confession. In classical liberal arts education, they have discovered a model developed by the church that is supportive of the faith and has proven itself in time-tested ways to be superior to anything that the current educational establishment can offer. This is not just an educational fad. As the movement has matured, it has developed responsible standards, engaged in thoughtful academic research, and instituted rigorous teacher training programs.

The classical liberal arts education model is incredibly adaptable to a wide variety of circumstances. Many independent Christian classical schools are situated in affluent neighborhoods where parents can afford the tuition required for private education. Perhaps because of this, the charge is sometimes unfairly made that classical liberal arts education is elitist. In the Lutheran church, classical education has been successfully used in almost every conceivable socioeconomic environment because schools are most often connected to the local parish. It has been implemented effectively by schools in rural Illinois, suburban Virginia, small cities in Wyoming, and urban Texas. One of the first Lutheran classical schools was established by an urban church in Ft. Wayne, Indiana in which a strong majority of students were from economically disadvantaged households. My own experience was with a school in rural northern Ontario where levels of educational and economic achievement were well below the national average. The point is that children are children, teaching is teaching, and classical liberal arts education is effective in every setting. While the approach that each of these schools has taken is different, they have adapted the model to the unique needs and challenges of the local community. At the same time, there is a striking uniformity that comes from a shared confession of faith and a desire to make that confession the normative force behind everything that is done in the school. School boards and faculty are relentless in asking the question, "Is this consistent with what we teach, believe, and confess?"

In these schools, students are treated with a level of respect engendered by the pedagogy itself. Students are co-heirs with Christ and deserve to be taught the wisdom that comes from him and benefits them spiritually, emotionally, and academically. Their standing as children of the eternal, timeless God dictates that they be taught matters of eternal and timeless worth. This stands in contrast to the educational models promoted by the government which are comparatively resource-intensive and rely on the latest educational technology and software. Teachers need constant updating and retraining so that they can implement the most current learning strategies and curricula. Classrooms have to be equipped to accommodate "active learning" and meet the needs of an endless variety of learning styles. The reality for Christian educators who try to emulate or adapt a government sanctioned model is that many schools—especially parish schools—simply don't have the resources to do this. As a result, they are under-resourced imitators of their public school counterparts. One of the practical advantages of classical liberal arts education is that resources are relatively accessible and inexpensive. At its core, all a classically-styled classroom requires is a good teacher, a few good books, and some pens and paper. Obviously, classical liberal arts education does not reject the use of technology in the classroom or good teaching aids. I have seen some classical schools use technologies that were not even available in many public schools. It is not that classical education rejects technology. It just does not depend on it: it is secondary to the pedagogical model. This makes classical liberal arts education adaptable for use in parish schools with limited resources, small school cooperatives, and homeschool families. It also makes it a particularly attractive model for educators in developing countries, where resources are limited and technological support is scarce.

A shift to the church's historic model of education has dramatic implications for teachers. Because the curriculum is content-rich, teachers need to be masters of what they are teaching, knowing their material well enough so that they can discriminate between good content and poor content. The state's hostility to the aims of Christian education makes this skill all the more essential. Teachers also need to know theology and Christian pedagogy well enough to assess whether or not both content and methods conform to the wisdom of Christ, the goals of Evangelical education, and the confessions of the church. That is a difficult thing to do, and there is no metric to assess competency in this area. Yet, for a true Evangelical teacher, it is one of the most essential skills.[1]

This is not to say that teachers should ignore developments in teaching methods and the like. Occasionally, the charge is made that classical liberal arts education rejects all innovations. My experience has been the opposite. Teachers tend to carefully examine classroom materials and teaching methods to see if they align with the overall philosophy and theology of Christian education.

Implementing a classical pedagogy program in an existing school is not an easy thing to do. The old adage "change is never easy" is never truer than when it comes to jettisoning ideas and methods that have become entrenched in our educational consciousness. Yet that is what is required. There needs to be a dispassionate evaluation of the entire nature of Christian education with the goal of reworking it to make it truly and thoroughly Christian. Parents, school boards, staff, and school supporters have to be committed to enacting the required changes. Make no mistake—implementing a classical model of education is hard work. There are no shortcuts. Those involved with the school must be prepared for this reality. Parents need to realize that there will be increased expectations from the students. School boards need to be comfortable with the fact that it will often take years before the new culture of learning will be the norm. Supporters must be patient, understanding that their investment will return dividends only years down the road. The dividends, however, will be well worth the investment.

A recent study conducted by the University of Notre Dame Sociology Department on behalf of the Association of Classical Christian Schools compared alumni of six different school types. The survey revealed that the alumni of classical schools "think and live in a markedly different way than their peers from other educational models. Nearly 90% of them attend church at least 3 times monthly, and they participate in other church activities at a higher rate. They are 2.6 times more likely to pray alone and 6.7 times more likely to be readers." Graduates were far more likely than their peers to accept the authority of the church while at the same time having a high regard for science. As a result, they were more likely than any other group to view science and religion as being compatible. Against the charge that a classical liberal arts education squelches healthy critical thinking, the study also revealed that, while they were more likely to remain faithful, they still questioned their faith. The study also concludes that they have "much lower divorce and cohabitation rates compared to other groups" and are "the best prepared academically, more than double the next highest group."[2]

The validity of the church's pedagogy should be anchored in its theological integrity and not in statistical results. That said, these findings really shouldn't come as a surprise. If children have been trained with rigor and in intellectual humility, then it is only natural that they would be more likely to submit to the authority of the Word and to one another. And if children have been taught to love that which is timeless, then it is only natural that they would grow up and love the one God who "was in the beginning, is now, and ever shall be."

I suspect that a good number of Christian teachers already sense a disconnect between the prevailing models of education and their confession of faith and harbor a desire for something better.[3] Such self-evaluation is difficult, but worthwhile. Doing so will reveal that there is indeed a model of education that allows them to do what they wanted to do when they first went into teaching—shape young minds with the wisdom of Christ.

Colleges of education in Christian colleges and universities also must be ready to critically evaluate the pedagogies that are promoted. Here I make a special appeal to my education colleagues to join in an exploration of how the church's confession shapes teacher education.

This is not an easy paradigm shift. It will involve transitioning away from the traditional emphasis on methods' classes by cultivating teachers who desire excellent content and sound theology. It means replacing the standard canon of modern secular educators with the great Christian pedagogues of history. Future teachers have to be taught not to rely on a preset curriculum, but to know their topic so well that they can create the appropriate lessons for teaching the material. This, not state licensure, is what makes for a well-qualified teacher. This measurement dates back over two millennia. The Roman educator Quintilian said,

> It is the best possible reason for handing over a boy to the best teachers that with them the pupils, being better taught, will either say what is worth imitating or will be corrected at once, if they make a mistake. But an ignorant teacher will perhaps even give his approval to what is faulty and through his judgement upon it commend it to his hearers. The teacher, then, should be outstanding alike in eloquence and moral character, able like Phoenix in Homer to teach his pupils both how to speak and how to act.[4]

In the sixteenth and seventeenth centuries, hundreds of school orders were written for schools in Evangelical territories. These orders generally had no prescribed curricula, testing standards, model lesson plans, or desired learning outcomes. They did not mandate that teachers attend special colleges or take age- or subject-specific methods classes. In short, they did not prescribe the very things that drive so much of contemporary government-run education. What received the most attention in these orders was the confession and character of the teacher. They emphasized the importance of teachers being virtuous, leading wholesome lives, having the right confession of faith, and holding to the true doctrine. Teachers were to be well-read, have a love of learning, and love their students. The formulators of the school orders understood that, in order to have wise and eloquent students, they needed wise and eloquent teachers. I am not suggesting that we attempt to reconstitute the schools of the sixteenth century or any other historical period. The world in which we live is very different. We have different experiences and perspectives both of what we know and how we understand children. What I am suggesting is that we return to the fundamental principles of Christian education—the source of which is found in the great teachers of the past—and use those as the basis for building a path forward.

The era of seeking government approval of the church's teachers must be put to rest. We don't seek state approval for our pastors or deaconesses, parish musicians, or directors of Christian education. To do so would be an insult to them. It would say that the training they received from the church was insufficient for them to conduct their calling. We should accord the same dignity to our teachers. Christian teachers love Christ's wisdom, learning about it, and teaching it. For this reason, the church—not the state—is the sole agency qualified to endorse such teachers.

Conclusion

In the fourteenth century, the Ottoman Sultan, Murad I, formed an elite ruthless fighting force called the Janissaries. This army—one of the first standing armies in Europe—was made up of men who had been kidnapped as boys from Christian families by Ottoman raiding parties. The boys were given to Muslim parents, taught the Turkish languages, raised to be devout Muslims, and taught to hate Christians. Upon completing their training, they were made to swear an oath of complete loyalty to the sultan and often, in order to prove their loyalty, these Janissaries were sent back to their home villages to slaughter their own people.

For almost a century now, Christians have unwittingly been giving their children over to be raised as spiritual and intellectual "Janissaries." They have been spiritually kidnapped "through philosophy and empty deceit based on human traditions, based on the elements of the world rather than on Christ" (Col 2:8). They have been tutored with pedagogies designed to destroy the Christian faith into which they were baptized. They have been spiritually and morally removed from their families and molded according to the edicts of state-sponsored "educrats." They have been taught to forget the language of faith and speak only the language of unbelief. They have been taught the piety and devotion of Gnosticism and Secular Liberalism. For the better part of a century, we have welcomed these pedagogies of enslavement into Christian schools with the mistaken belief that they had no particular theological bias or spiritual agenda. Worried that we would lose children to state-run schools, we tried to mimic those schools believing that, if we could do what "they" were doing—with perhaps the addition of a religion class and a chapel service—then our schools would be just as attractive. It was an experiment that failed.

This book is a call for the church to go on the educational offensive by reclaiming her own distinct way of educating children. This way is time-tested, adaptable, and academically superior to most anything that is offered in contemporary secular education. Most importantly, it is theologically sound. It meets the needs of the church and forms young Christian minds so that they can readily receive the Word preached to them and cling to the sacraments offered to them. What is the downside to going down this path when there is the possibility that we might just raise up a new generation with the intellectual and doctrinal prowess to lead the church forward in these troubling times?

This is no easy thing, but good Christian education never has been. This history of Christian education is filled with complaints about a lack of adequate teachers, insufficient funds, poorly motivated students, and intrusive, disgruntled, or apathetic parents. But this should not stop us from seeking something better. Just because there has never been a golden age of education does not mean we should ignore the fact that the church of the past had something that we have lost: a classical model of liberal arts education.

I believe that we are at the beginning of a recovery of that model. The past 20 years of the classical education movement has been exciting, and some enormous strides have been made; however, what is to come will be even more impressive. Academic research is needed to direct and inform this movement. Colleges and universities need to concentrate on training teachers who excel academically and theologically. Structured assistance has to be provided to schools and congregations seeking to recover this heritage. Parents—especially homeschool parents—require resources, support, and advocacy as they reclaim their divinely mandated role as the primary teachers of their children. It is daunting for sure, but I am convinced that the church, as the holy body of Christ, will rise to the task just has she has in the past.

* * *

For bringing up their children properly is their shortest road to heaven. In fact heaven itself could not be made nearer or achieved more easily than by doing this work....You could do no more disastrous work than to spoil the children, let them curse and swear, let them learn profane words and vulgar songs, and just let them do as they please...There is no greater tragedy in Christendom than spoiling children. If we want to help Christendom, we most certainly have to start with the children, as happened in earlier times. "[1]

Appendices

Appendix 1: Comparison of Classical Christian Education and Liberal Education

Liberal education is the prevailing paradigm used in education today. It grew out of a secular view of man and the world which sought to divorce education from theology, and thereby marginalize religion. A renewed interest in classical Christian education has developed over the past several decades. It draws inspiration from the liberal arts model of education that was used by the church to educate children for almost two millennia. It seeks to develop a model of education that supports and promotes a Confessional Christian worldview.

	Classical Christian Education *Looking to God in faith and to one's neighbor in love.*	Liberal (Constructionist, Discovery, Authentic, Progressive) *"Participation of the individual in the social consciousness of the race."*—John Dewey
Nature of Child	The child is a sinner that has been redeemed by Christ.	Sin is denied. The wrong that a child commits has been learned from external influences (society, parents, etc.).

Nature of Truth	All truth comes from God. This includes the saving truth of Christ which is revealed only in Scriptures, and the truth which has been revealed to men outside of Scriptures.	Truth is the construction of the individual and/or community. It is often connected with issues of power/oppression.
Objectives	Wisdom. Students are taught subjects that are practical and applicable to what it means to be human. Life is more than work and material goods. All students will profit best from understanding how the whole of life fits together, knowing that the great ideas of the past will enable them to better understand human nature.	Vocational/Technical. Students are taught subject matter which is deemed to be applicable and practical, primarily in terms of what will help them to land a good-paying job. The school-to-work philosophy maintains that the goal of education is to place children in the work force so that they may be good producers and consumers of marketable items.
Teacher's Role	Teachers are the source of knowledge and authority figures (4th Commandment). They are expected to master subject matter.	Teachers act as facilitators, counselors, and mentors. Mastery of teaching methods is valued above content.
Instruction	Direct instruction by the teacher in homogeneous groups (groups of students with similar abilities). There is a focus on intellectual, factual learning. Rote memory is encouraged, especially in younger children. Facts are the raw material of thought and the building blocks for future learning.	Student (self-directed) learning, discovery learning, and cooperative work in heterogeneous groups. Learning is viewed as a process of forming new relationships within the community. There is a focus on personal feelings, interpretations, and opinions. Rote memory is discouraged as it is seen to hinder free thought.

Curriculum	The curriculum focuses on academic areas with facts, ideas, skills, and methods that include student discovery. The course of studies is seen as a continuous whole from Pre-K through University, understanding that knowledge builds on knowledge. There is a clear picture of what a student will have at the end of his term at the academy. All classes are taught with that goal in mind.	There is little unity across subject matters. Each subject is treated in isolation. Students are encouraged to give preference to the perspectives of the "marginalized" as they are understood to be more "authentic."
Critical Thinking	Critical Thinking is not isolated from its content. Students learn to think mathematically, geographically, theologically, and scientifically. They are given the tools of logic to develop arguments based on the information that they have learned.	Critical Thinking is used as a code word in which students must first reject all authorities (including the 1st and 4th Commandment) and then appropriate only what they deem to be right for themselves. It is taught as a skill that can be naturally mastered without reference to content or established rules of logic.
Outcomes	Emphasis on academic skills in traditional core areas, measured objectively.	Emphasis on the "whole child" approach that blends psychological, social and cultural well-being of the child, measured subjectively.
Character Development	Service to one's neighbor according to one's vocation. Self-control and humility.	Relativism (no right or wrong) and self-esteem. Emphasis on self-actualization and ability to think critically (a rejection of all previously assumed paradigms and structures).

Appendix 2: J. C. Vonderau's Learn-by-Heart Schedule for Hymns[1]

Table 1: Hymns Included in the *Liederpensum*

Hymn #[2]	German First Line	English First Line[3]
2	Ach bleib' mit deiner Gnade	Abide, O dearest Jesus
28	Laßt uns alle fröhlich sein	Let us all with gladsome voice
37	Nun singet und seid froh	Now sing we, now rejoice
41, sts. 1–6, 13	Vom Himmel hoch, da komm' ich her	From heav'n above to earth I come
49	Das neugeborne Kindelein	The new-born Child this early morn
84, sts. 9–10	O Haupt voll Blut und Wunden	O sacred Head, now wounded
86	O Lamm Gottes unschuldig	Lamb of God, pure and holy
95	Wir danken dir, Herr Jesu Christ	Lord Jesus, we give thanks to Thee
97	Auf, auf mein Herz, mit Freuden	Awake, my heart, with gladness
117	Auf Christi Himmelfahrt allein	On Christ's ascension I now build
134	Komm, Heiliger Geist, Herre Gott	Come, Holy Ghost, God, and Lord!
145	Gott, der Vater, wohn uns bei	God the Father, be our Stay
158	Ein feste Burg ist unser Gott	A mighty Fortress is our God
159	Erhalt, uns, Herr, bei deinem Wort, und steur	Lord, Keep us in Thy Word and work
174, st. 1	Laß mich dein sein und bleiben	Let me be Thine forever
223	Jetzt ist dir Gnadenzeit	Now is the time of grace
229	So wahr ich Lebe, spricht dein Gott	Yea, as I live, thy Maker saith

234	Aus Gnaden soll ich selig werden	By grace I'm saved, grace free and boundless
254	Meinen Jesum lass ich nicht, denn er ist allein	Jesus I will never leave
270	Herr wie du willst, so schick's mit mir	Lord, as Thou wilt, deal Thou with me
297	Gott des Himmels und der Erden	God who madest earth and heaven
317	Hinunter ist der Sonnenschein	The sun's last beam of light is gone
319, st. 8	Nun ruhen alle Wälder	Now rest beneath night's shadow
324	Fang dein Werk mit Jesu an	With the Lord begin thy task
333	Mein lieber Gott, ich bitte dich	Dear God, I pray Thee, graciously
336	Bis hieher hat mich Got gebracht durch seine groß Güte	The Lord hath helped me hitherto
341	Lobe den Herren, den mächtigen König der Ehren	Praise to the Lord, the Almighty
346	Nun danket alle Gott	Now thank we all our God
355	Befiehl du deine Wege und was dein Herze kränkt	Commit whatever grieves thee
362	Hilf, Helfer, hilf in Angst und Not, Erbarm' dich	Help, Helper help, in fear and need
376	Was Gott thut, das ist wohlgethan!	What God ordains is always good
382	Wer nur den lieben Gott läßt walten	If thou but suffer God to guide thee
111, sts. 1–6	JEsus, meine Zuversicht	Jesus Christ, my sure Defense
412 st. 1	In Christi Wunden schlaf ich ein	I fall asleep in Jesus' wounds
433	Es ist gewißlich an der Zeit	The day is surely drawing near

Table 2: Hymn Assignments per Classroom

Classroom	I.	II.	II.	III.	III.	IV.
Grade	[I.] II.	III.	IV.	V.	VI.	VII. VIII.
	28 41, 13. 95, 1. 2. 223 554, 1. 297, 1. 2. 319, 8. 333 362	41, 1–4. 95, 3. 4. 117, 1. 174, 1. 234, 1. 254, 2. 3. 297, 3. 4. 317 324, 1. 2. 341, 1. 2.	41, 5. 6. 86 49 117, 2. 234, 2. 3. 254, 4–6. 297, 5–7. 324, 3–5, 341, 3–5.	37 97, 1–4. 117, 3. 145 234, 4. 5. 111, 1–6. 346 159	84, 9. 10. 97, 5–9. 158 2, 3–6. 355 336	134 229 270 376 382 433 234, 6–10.
		412, 1. 2, 1. 2.				
# of stanzas to learn	19	21	22	26	30	38*
# of stanzas repeated	—	19	40	62	88	118
Total learned	19	40	62	88	118	156

* "There are also a number of psalms and important passages from the Bible that cannot be found in the catechism."[4]

Appendix 3: Matching Hymns for the Six Chief Parts of Luther's Small Catechism and the Augsburg Confession

This was compiled by Mr. Ted Lams, Principal Emeritus, St. Paul Lutheran School, Brookfield, IL, for use in 7th & 8th grade. It is an example of an integrated approach to catechesis and music.

The Six Chief Parts of Luther's Small Catechism

	Lutheran Service Book	*The Lutheran Hymnal*
The Ten Commandments	581	287
The Creed	954	251
The Lord's Prayer	766	458
Holy Baptism	406 (Christ Unser Herr)	300 (Liebster Jesu)
Confession and Absolution	607	329
Sacrament of the Altar	627	311

The Augsburg Confession

Article # Article Title *Lutheran Service Book*

I	The Creeds	954
II	Original Sin	608, 562
III	The Son of God	332, 333, 382, 402
IV	Justification	492, 555-577, 596
V	Pastoral Office	589, 681
VI	Sanctification	685, 688, 689, 693, 694, 696, 722, 730
VII & VIII	The Christian Church	644, 645, 909, 912
IX	Baptism	405, 406
X & XIII	The Sacraments	617, 622, 623, 625, 627, 628, 636
XI & XII	Confession and Repentance	562, 608, 704, 755, 942
XIV	Of Ecclesiastical Order	589, 681
XV	Human Traditions	See "Reformation" Hymns
XVI	Of Political Order	505, 717, 965
XVII	The Lord's Return	See "Advent" Hymns
XVIII	Free Will	See "Sanctification" Hymns
XIX	The Cause of Sin	561, See "Lent" Hymns
XX	Faith & Good Works	555, 556, 557, 559, 562, 568
XXI	The Cult of Saints	766, 909
XXII & XXVIII	Correction of Abuses	No Specific Hymns

Notes

Introduction

1 "Classical Lutheran Education Defined," Institute for the Lutheran Liberal Arts, accessed January 05, 2020, http://illa.us. Joel Brondos defines Classical Lutheran Education in the following way. "We teach children to look to God in faith and to care for their neighbor in love by means of the Six Chief Parts and the Seven Liberal Arts."

Part I Bitten by the Snake

How Theology Shapes Pedagogy

1 Gustav Pinzger, *Valentin Friedland Trotzendorf dargestellt. Mit Trotzendorfs Bildniss und Facsimile seiner Handschrift* (Hirschberg, 1825).
2 The work of scientist philosophers like that of Richard Dawkins and Steven Hawking should be sufficient to put an end to that argument, for in no way are they theologically neutral. Their theories are directly shaped by their confession that there is no god and that we are the masters of our own destiny.
3 "10 of the Best Growth Mindset Activities for Kids," no. July 09, 2020. https://wabisabilearning.com/blogs/mindfulness-wellbeing/growth-mindset-activities-kids.
4 Philip Schaff and Henry Wace, *A Select library of Nicene and post-Nicene fathers of the Christian church. Second series*, 14 vols., vol. II (New York: The Christian Literature Company, 1890), 545.
5 Martin Luther, "To the Christian Nobility," *LW* 44:207.

6 Johann Heinrich Pestalozzi, *The Education of Man*, trans. William H. Kilpatrick (New York: Greenwood Press, 1969), 90.
7 Friedrich Froebel, "Education of Man," in *Friedrich Froebel: A Selection from His Writings* (London: Cambridge University Press, 1967), 57.
8 Kieran Egan, *Getting It Wrong from the Beginning: Our Progressivist Inheritance from Herbert Spencer, John Dewey, and Jean Piaget* (New Haven: Yale University Press, 2002), 14.
9 Herbert Spencer, *Essays on Education and Kindred Subjects,* ed. Ernest Rhys Essays, (London: J. M. Dent & Sons, 1916), 62.
10 Spencer, *Essays on Education and Kindred Subjects*, 62.
11 "Humanist Manifesto," 1933, accessed November 24, 2019, https://americanhumanist.org/what-is-humanism/manifesto1/.
12 These ideas were common to people such as Rudolf Steiner (founder of the Waldorf schools), the English educational reformer Charlotte Mason, and Maria Montessori. Robert Baden-Powell, founder of the Boy Scout Movement, also based many of his ideas on this romantic view.
13 John Dewey, "My Pedagogic Creed," *School Journal* 54, no. January (1897), 1897. 77-80
14 Dewey, "My Pedagogic Creed." 77-80
15 The irony of this is that Dewey is guilty of doing the very thing he accuses the church of. He identifies Christians as false teachers and he divides the world between the "saved," the enlightened followers of his new theology of secularism, and the "damned," those who hold to the Christian confession.
16 John Dewey, *The Human Nature and Conduct: An Introduction to Social Psychology* (New York: Henry Holt, 1922), 331.
17 Dewey, *The Human Nature and Conduct*, 330.
18 W. F. Warde, "The Fate of Dewey's Theories," *International Socialist Review* 21, no. 2 (1960): 31, https://www.marxists.org/archive/novack/works/1960/x04.htm. Dewey's view of science is consistent with those of many late 19th century intellectuals who believed that the burgeoning field of science could (and would) solve all of mankind problems. Herbert Spencer stated "What knowledge is of most worth? –the uniform reply is—Science. This is the verdict on all counts. For direct self-preservation, or the maintenance of life and health, the all-important knowledge is—Science." Herbert Spencer, "The Importance of Science," in *Readings in the History of Education*, ed. Ellwood P. Cubberly (Chicago: Houghton Mifflin, 1920). 650
19 Warde, "The Fate of Dewey's Theories," 8.
20 John Dewey, "Impressions of Soviet Russia," in *John Dewey: The Later Works*, ed. Jo Ann Boydston (Carbondale: Southern Illinois University) 212.
21 Dewey, "Impressions of Soviet Russia," 241.

22 Dewey, "My Pedagogic Creed." 77-80
23 Dewey, "My Pedagogic Creed."
24 Dewey, "My Pedagogic Creed."
25 Some in the educational world have turned on this "Father of Progressive Education" for being too regressive. One scholar criticizes Dewey as being an unwitting puppet of the 19th century capitalists. In his view, Dewey's pedagogy was designed to produce materialistic citizens who would surrender their individualism in support of a capitalist industrial society. See Chet Bowers, *Education for Eco-Justice and Community* (Athens, Georgia: University of Georgia Press, 2001). In another more radical critique, it is claimed that "Dewey's educational theories continue to be relevant today because the same capitalistic system continues." This is followed by a call to get rid of capitalism all together. "A Marxist Critique of John Dewey: The Limits of Progressive Education," Left Voice, 2017, accessed May 05, 2021, https://www.leftvoice.org/a-marxist-critique-of-john-dewey-the-limits-of-progressive-education/.
26 Stephen Toulmin, "The Mozart of Psychology," Book Review, *New York Times*, September 28, 1979.
27 Educationalists and psychologists, in an effort to defend Vygotsky, argue that his ideas were rejected by Stalin and that his writings were banned by his administration. Some historians have pointed out that there is little to support this assertion. Far from being a threat to Stalin, Vygotsky rose to prominence during Stalin's rule, he was given positions of prestige during the worst of the Stalinist purges, and after his death of natural causes, he was buried in a cemetery reserved for Soviet heroes. Jennifer Fraser and Anton Yasnitsky, "Deconstructing Vygotsky's Victimization Narrative: A Re-examination of the 'Stalinist suppression' of Vygotskian Theory," *History of the Human Sciences* 28, no. 2 (2015), https://doi.org/10.1177/0952695114560200.
28 L. S. Vygotsky et al., *The Essential Vygotsky* (New York: Kluwer Academic/Plenum Publishers, 2004), 342.
29 Lunacharsky was impressed with Vygotsky and was instrumental in bringing him to Moscow and giving him the resources to carry out his work. It was Lunacharsky who invited John Dewey to tour the Soviet Union in 1927 and who was eager to implement many of Dewey's educational ideas. See Warde, "The Fate of Dewey's Theories."
30 Guenter Lewy, *If God Is Dead Everything Is Permitted* (New Brunswick, NJ: Transaction Publishers, 2008), 62.
31 Martin Luther, "Lectures on Romans" *LW*, 25:345
32 Vygotsky drew on the ideas of the nineteenth-century philosopher, Friedrich Nietzsche, who believed that the Übermensch—or

superman—was the next step in the evolutionary process. While Nietzsche saw this primarily as a biological evolution, Vygotsky understood that this new man was the result of social evolution L. S. Vygotsky, "The Socialist Alteration of Man," ed. Rene van der Veer and Jaan Valsiner, *Vygotsky Reader* (Blackwell, 1930), https://www.marxists.org/archive/vygotsky/works/1930/socialism.htm.. This new man would not be beholden to religious superstition, but would create meaning and purpose appropriate for himself. While Christianity looks to the world to come as the only hope for this life, Nietzsche believed that hope could only be found in this life and in the inevitable progress of mankind toward a new superior human being. Not only was this idea influential in Marxism, but it was also the basis for the Nazi's interest in the Aryan super race.

33 L. S. Vygotsky, "Educational Psychology," trans. Robert Silverman (Florida: St. Lucie Press, 1926), https://www.marxists.org/archive/vygotsky/works/1926/educational-psychology/index.htm.

34 Jaime Budzienski, "Activities to Teach Toddlers With Vygotsky's Theory," (October 30, 2014 2014). https://howtoadult.com/activities-teach-toddlers-vygotskys-theory-16606.html.

35 Vygotsky, "Educational Psychology."

36 Vygotsky, "Educational Psychology."

37 Lucien Sève, "Where is Marx in the Work and Thought of Vygotsky" (7e Seminaire International Vygotski, 20-22 juin 2018 2018). Interestingly there the educational establishment has raised few questions about the academic honesty of this. One could surmise that the translators saw this as an opportunity to surreptitiously introduce Marxist ideology into American education thought.

38 Dave Hill, "Marxist Education Against Capitalism in Neoliberal/Neoconservative Times," in *Marxism and Education*, ed. L. Rasinski, D. Hill and K. Skordoulis (New York: Routledge, 2018).

39 Michigan K-12 Standards: English Language Arts, 23.

40 "About Montessori Education," American Montessori Association, accessed July 01, 2020, https://amshq.org/About-Montessori.

41 Montessori never adequately addressed the issue of how children could have an interest in something they have never been exposed to. What appears to be a "natural interest" may be restricted by their environment, culture, and limited experience. For example, how is a child to pursue language study if he or she has never been exposed to another language? I often have upper-level university students who regret they did not take Latin and Greek earlier in their schooling. No one ever thought to give them exposure to the languages and so they never thought of learning them.

NOTES 127

42 In her writings Montessori rarely makes any reference to her affiliation with the Roman Catholic Church. She was so private that many of her disciples failed to make any connection.
43 Montessori writes as though the soul of a child preexisted its conception. In a chapter called "The Spiritual Embryo" she talks about a child's spirit being "enclosed in flesh when it comes to live in the world." She likens it to being in a "dark dungeon striving to come out into the light, to be born…and which slowly but surely animates the sluggish flesh." Maria Montessori, *The Secret of Childhood*, trans. Joseph Costelloe (Indiana: Fides Publishers, 1966), 35-44.
44 Maria Montessori, *Education and Peace*, trans. Helen Lane (Chicago: Henry Regnery, 1972), 86.
45 Montessori, *Education and Peace*, 104.
46 Maria Montessori, *To Educate the Human Potential* (Madras, India: Kalakshetra Publications, 1955), 34.
47 Maria Montessori, *The Absorbent Mind* (Oxford, England: Clio Press, 1988), 248.
48 Many of Piaget's "objective" observations came from watching his own children.
49 Piaget's own training was not in psychology but in zoology, having earned a doctorate in Natural Sciences from University of Neuchâtel.
50 Michael Chapman, *Constructive Evolution: Origins and Development of Piaget's Thought* (New York: Cambridge University Press, 1988), 70. http://www.loc.gov/catdir/description/cam023/87021816.html.
51 Chapman, *Constructive Evolution*, 72.
52 Fernado Vidal, *Piaget Before Piaget* (Cambridge, Mass: Harvard University Press, 1994), 52.
53 Quoted in Eric Shiraev, *A History of Psychology* (Washington: Sage, 2011), 240.
54 Quoted in Lynn S. Liben, *Piaget and the Foundations of Knowledge*, The Jean Piaget Symposium series, (Hillsdale, N.J.: L. Erlbaum Associates, 1983), 145.
55 Webster Callaway, *Jean Piaget: A Most Outrageous Deception* (New York: Nova Science Publishers, 2001), 91.

The Venom of Liberal Education

1 The fact that the term "Enlightenment" is still used by academics reveals a particular bias. It conveys the thought that before Rousseau and the Enlightenment people were ignorant. They lived in the "Dark Ages" during which they trusted in God, believed the church, and understood

Scriptures as truth. With the Enlightenment, truth came to light and we now realize that we no longer need the teachings of faith.

2 The use of the term "sciences" does not refer to the modern sciences. Classically there were three categories of sciences: the natural sciences (natural philosophy), the inquiry about human nature (moral philosophy) and theology (divine philosophy).

3 Mark C. Carnes and Gary Kates, *Rousseau, Burke and revolution in France, 1791*, "Reacting to the past" series, (New York: Pearson Longman, 2005), 70.

4 Carnes and Kates, *Rousseau, Burke and revolution in France, 1791*, 74.

5 Jean Jacques Rousseau, *The Social Contract*, trans. Charles Frankel (New York: Hafner Publishing, 1947).

6 Jean Jacques Rousseau, *Social Contract and Discourses* (New York: Dutton, 1913), https://www.bartleby.com/168/.

7 The French Revolution, which was inspired by many of the early Enlightenment thinkers offers a realistic illustration as to where such "natural impulses" lead. The chaos, violence, and bloodshed that was committed in the name of the great Enlightenment ideal should cause one to question the wisdom of advocating for the incorporation of Rousseau's beliefs in any educational model.

8 Levinson is willing to grant that parents and Christian schools are capable of inculcating children with a proper sense of autonomy but only if they first align themselves with the goals of state sponsored liberal education. See Meira Levinson, *The demands of liberal education* (New York: Oxford University Press, 1999).

9 Far from being regarded an extremist by the educational establishment this Harvard professor received the 2013 Exemplary Research in Social Studies Award by the National Council for the Social Studies and the American Educational Studies Association Critics Choice Award for her book *No Citizen Left Behind*.

10 Walter Feinberg, "Religious Education in Liberal Democratic Societies: The Question of Accountability and Autonomy," in *Education and Citizenship in Liberal-Democratic Societies: Teaching for Cosmopolitan Values and Collective Identities*, ed. Kevin McDonough and Walter Feinberg (Oxford: Oxford University Press, 2003). Levinson, Feinberg is highly regard for his work and in 2014 received a "Lifetime Achievement" award from the John Dewey Society.

11 Erin O'Donnell, "The Risks of Homeschooling," *Harvard Magazine*, no. May-June 2020 (2020). https://www.harvardmagazine.com/2020/05/right-now-risks-homeschooling.

12 The myth lies at the core of the Gnostic elevation of the feminine qualities of spirituality, the rejection of marriage, and the support of radical

feminism. Gnostic promoter and Princeton professor Elaine Pagels argues that the natural desire of a woman for a man within the confines of marriage is seen as a reflection of this original sin. She believes that the Gnostics were not heretics who denied the faith, but genuine Christians who had a greater insight and whose views were unduly suppressed by orthodox theologians. Elaine Pagels, *Adam, Eve, and the Serpent* (New York: Random House, 1988).

13 Mike Mitchell and Walt Dohrn, "Trolls," (2016).
14 Peter Burfeind, *Gnostic America* (Pax Domini Press, 2014), 123-24. For an extended exploration of the Gnostic influence in American culture, I recommend this book.
15 This is not to say that educators shouldn't want students to develop a love of independent learning. To the contrary, Christian educators throughout history have recognized its value and have sought to develop this desire in their students. The difference is that, classically, this love of learning has been achieved by giving students what the teacher has first learned to be the most beneficial. Students have to know what is good and worth learning before they can explore by themselves.
16 Because of its inability to rely on words to convey truth and wisdom, Gnostic-influenced education has condemned itself to being intellectually bankrupt. In the long-run, it is incapable of defending itself against arguments based on a transcendent truth. This fact alone should make the educator question the wisdom in promoting its philosophy.
17 Samael Aun Weor, *Fundamentals of Gnostic Education* (Brooklyn NY: Glorian, 2013), Kindle.
18 Weor, *Fundamentals of Gnostic Education*, 450-51.
19 Weor, *Fundamentals of Gnostic Education*, 629-34.
20 Weor, *Fundamentals of Gnostic Education*, 453-55.

Striking Where It Hurts

1 The nineteenth-century German educational reformers would prove especially influential in the development of twentieth-century American educational philosophies. The ideas of German educationalists such as Pestalozzi, Wilhelm Humboldt (1767-1835), and Johann Herbart (1776-1841) would all be taken up by American educationalists who admired the German educational system. Some, such as Friedrich Froebel, the founder of Kindergarten, were outright rejected by his contemporary countrymen but were warmly received by American intellectual elites. These educators prepared the way for the introduction of Marxist, Gnostic, Mystic and Liberal Education in the twentieth century.

2. Plato, *The Republic*, trans. Benjamin Jowett (Mineola, New York: Dover, 2000), 52. also "We will not have them trying to persuade our youth that the gods are the authors of evil, and that heroes are no better than men—sentiments which, as we were saying, are neither pious nor true, for we have already proved that evil cannot come from the gods…they [false teachers] are likely to have a bad effect on those who hear them for everybody will begin to excuse his own vices when he is convinced that similar wickednesses are always being perpetuated by [such gods]," 63.
3. Scientism should not be confused with scientific findings. Scientism is the teaching that science is the only real knowledge that one can trust. More than just a set of findings, it is a view of the world which determines the value placed on those facts and how they are to be interpreted. I call it a religious system because it bears many of the marks that one would expect from a religion. It has a community of faithful; it has a "priesthood" charged with maintaining a type of doctrinal purity. It regards science as the source of ethics and maintains that science will provide a salvation from all the ills that beset mankind. In spite of these religious-like marks, advocates of science will dogmatically assert that religion—especially the Christian religion—is the least reliable source for a knowledge of the truth.
4. The Greeks believed that the senses were inherently unreliable. Plato argued that sensory perception could always be deceived and was not only incapable of leading one to true wisdom, but often got in the way of that pursuit. Philosophy was required to correct the senses. Today's dabblers of natural and social science claim the opposite. The only trustworthy source of knowledge is that which can be perceived by the senses, and we cannot trust any other form of knowing.
5. Martin Luther, WA 48:31 quoted by Hermann Sasse, *Scripture and the Church: Select Essays of Hermann Sasse*, ed. Ronald R. Feuerhahn and Jeffery J. Kloha (St. Louis, MO: Concordia Seminary, 1995), 78.
6. The ancients understood poetry and philosophy to be intimately linked. The purpose of poetry was not just to evoke emotion. In fact, Plato warned about the danger of a society looking to its poets and artists for truth. It was a powerful tool for manipulating beliefs and opinions. Sound philosophy could be replaced by emotional appeal—a danger that is all too apparent in our entertainment-driven culture where performers believe that their artistic insights enable them to speak truth to the world like no one else. That said, poetry could be a tool to convey a philosophical argument in a way that prose could not. This understanding resurfaced during the Reformation. Philip Melanchthon saw philosophy as a natural extension of the Liberal Arts and believed that poetry should be philosophy arranged in verse form.

7 *LW* 54:210-211.
8 *LW* 36:342.
9 The answer to the reason behind the structure of the snowflake wouldn't be discovered for another 300 years when scientists began to understand the nature of crystalline structure. This discovery does not negate Kepler's central point. There is an underlying order and symmetry of all matter that cannot be explained. There is no reason that things have to be the way they are apart from the creative power of an orderly God.
10 Augustine, *On Christian Doctrine*, ed. Philip Schaff, trans. James Shaw, vol. 2, Nicene and Post-Nicene Fathers, (Buffalo, NY: Christian Literature Publishing, 1887).18.28.
11 One group of student teachers informed me that they were forbidden from playing dodgeball with the children because this was considered a "human targeting game". Undoubtedly some pedagogue somewhere developed a theory that mass murderers got their start playing dodge ball in third grade gym class.
12 The idea that children should be used as experimental subjects for a theorist's "innovative" methods should be repugnant to teachers and parents alike. It is shocking how often the educational establishment will push some "new approach" on students and, after it has proved to be a failure, simply move on to something else with little thought as to the damaging effects their irresponsible experimentation has had on the children who suffered through it.
13 The image of a teacher as a strict disciplinarian is a relatively recent concept. Its broad acceptance was encouraged by eighteenth-century pietism in which teachers were encouraged to use harsh discipline on students with the hope of mortifying their sinful impulses. Prior to that, virtually every Christian pedagogue, including Augustine and Luther, rejected the use of harsh discipline in the classroom as it was contrary to the task of teaching the pleasures of learning. Erasmus held that flogging was the sign of a weak teacher. Luther maintained that, while parents might well use corporal punishment, it should rarely ever be used by the school master.
14 To challenge these students I would ask them to list all the "atrocities" they could think of that were done in the name of the church throughout its entire history. Usually they could come up with the Spanish Inquisition and the Crusades–both of which they really knew little about. I would then ask them to start listing the atrocities that had been committed in the name of atheism or because of secular humanist teachings of the twentieth century (Holocaust, 6 million; Stalinist purges, 20 million; Mao's Cultural Revolution, 100 million; Cambodian Genocide, 2 million). They were almost all completely unaware of the violent persecution of the church under Hitler, Stalin, Mao or of any of the other persecutions of Christians

in the twentieth century. They soon realized that the greatest atrocities were committed not by the church but by the followers of philosophies that were intent on exterminating the church.
15 It is interesting how these same groups are all too happy to take copious amounts of money from the government to fund research into how western governments are so wicked. They seem to have no qualms about using government run schools as a launching pad for their assaults on supposedly evil governments.
16 LW 46:237.
17 LW 46: 237.
18 Katy Smith, "New Roles, New Relationships," *Educational Leadership* 51, no. 2 (1993).
19 Martin Luther, *What Luther Says: An Anthology*, ed. Ewald M. Plass, vol. I (St. Louis, MO: Concordia Publishing, 1959), 417. Weimar Edition 32:408
20 Consider how grading in a religion class subtly confuses Law and Gospel. If one receives an "A" does that mean that they are a superior Christian? If they receive an "F" what then does that mean?
21 James Fowler, the author of *Stages of Faith,* is perhaps the best known advocate of this.
22 LC 381
23 Bernard of Clairvaux Bernard, "Sermons on the Songs of Songs, Sermon 1," ed. Kilian Walsh, vol. 2, *The Works of Bernard of Clairvaux* (Kalamazoo, MI: Kalamazoo Publications, 1981), http://people.duke.edu/~dainotto/Texts/clairvaux.pdf.
24 LC 382
25 It is unfortunate that in Christian schools the holy task of catechizing children is reduced to a "Religion Class." The message that this conveys is that this is just like any other course and if a child learns enough knowledge about religion and the Bible then they have passed. It reinforces an understanding of the Christian faith as a mere intellectual exercise isolated from any sacramental connections.

The Effects

1 John M. Hull, "Atheism and the Future of Religious Education," in *Crossing the Boundaries: Essays in Biblical Interpretation in honour of Michael D. Goulder,* ed. Stanley Porter, Paul Joyce, and David Orton (Leiden: Brill, 1994).
2 *Millennials and Their Retention Since Confirmation*, Lutheran Church-Missouri Synod (2017), http://www.youthesource.com/wp-content

/uploads/2018/04/Millennials-Congregation-Confirmation-Survey-Report.pdf.
3. Speaking of Jobs' spiritual journey, one commentator remarked, "The irony is that Jobs became later in life exactly what he hated most about traditional Christian religion. The type of god that Job hated was exactly the god that Jobs himself became. What turned Jobs away from the alleged 'weaknesses' of Christianity, he blindly adopted himself." Austin Gentry, "Steve Jobs & Religion," August 19, 2016, https://www.austingentry.com/steve-jobs-religion/.
4. Obviously, we cannot limit God's ability to raise up brilliant theologians in an adverse educational environment; however, we should not try to impede His work with pedagogies that are contrary to His desires.

Part II Applying the Antidote

The Cure Of Timeless Standards

1. Measuring good in this way requires the acceptance that all things were created by God with a definite design and purpose. For this reason, modern educationalists neglect teaching goodness because that would require an acknowledgment that there is an authority higher than themselves. The same applies to the teaching of truth and beauty.
2. It is on this basis that my son argues that the Mazda Miata is the world's most perfect car and that he should have one.
3. Aristotle, "Metaphysics." http://classics.mit.edu/Aristotle/metaphysics.13.xiii.html.
4. Augustine, "The Literal Meaning of Genesis, Book III," in *Ancient Christian Writers Series*, ed. John Hammond Taylor (Paulist Press, 1982), 90.
5. Aristotle wrote, "To say of what is that it is not, or of what is not that it is, is false, while to say of what is that it is, and of what is not that it is not, is true." Aristotle, "Metaphysics."
6. XVI Benedict, *Jesus of Nazareth* (San Francisco: Ignatius Press, 2011).
7. The concept of different subjects that are distinct and unrelated is a relatively recent development. The ancients had divisions of knowledge but they understood that those divisions were simply aspects of the whole body of knowledge. Specializing in one area while remaining ignorant about other areas would have been considered the sign of a poorly educated man.
8. A similar term is used in 1 Peter 4:10 where Peter talks about the "varied grace of God." I am indebted to Rev. Chad Kendall for this observation.

9 David P. Scaer, "Doctrine of Election: A Lutheran Note," in *Perspectives on Evangelical Theology*, ed. Stanley N. Gundy (Indiana: Baker, 1979).
10 "What Is Classical Education?," accessed August 21, 2019, https://www.circeinstitute.org/resources/what-classical-education.
11 FC EP I, 16-17, 489-490.
12 FC EP II, 3, 492; this view is not restricted to the Book of Concord. The "Thirty Nine Articles of Religion" of the Anglican Communion state that "man is very far gone from original righteousness, and is of his own nature inclined to evil, so that the flesh lusteth always contrary to the Spirit; and therefore in every person born into this world it deserveth God's wrath and damnation" (Article IX) and "The condition of Man after the fall of Adam is such, that he cannot turn and prepare himself, by his own natural strength and good works, to faith, and calling upon God. Wherefore we have no power to do good works pleasant and acceptable to God, without the grace of God by Christ preventing us, that we may have a good will, and working with us, when we have that good will" (Article X). The Heidelberg Catechism asks "Can you keep all this [the Law of God] perfectly?" Answer" "No, I am inclined by nature to hate God and my neighbor."
13 On a trip to Pamplona, Spain, I visited some of the sites associated with the famous pilgrimage route, the *Camino Santiago*. In ancient times pilgrims would travel this route as a righteous work before God. Many modern day pilgrims still use it in this way. Though not viewed in religious terms, it is still a way for them to prove that they are among the good people. The difference is that in medieval times righteous acts were determined by the church—an external authority. Now they are assigned by the internal authority of self.
14 Frankforter, *The Theologia Germanica of Martin Luther*, ed. Bengt R. Hoffman, The Classics of Western spirituality, (New York: Paulist Press, 1980), 115.
15 Mark Mattes, *Martin Luther's Theology of Beauty: A Reappraisal* (Grand Rapids, MI: Baker Academic, 2017), 111.
16 Martin Luther, *Heidelberg Disputation* (Holt, MO: Higher Things Inc, 2018), 9. In 1518 Luther was called to Heidelberg to defend his theology before the leadership of the Augustinian order to which he belonged. For this disputation he composed a series of theses which described a theology of glory which centered on the works of man as a means to righteousness, and the theology of the cross which centered on the work of Christ for us. There is much in these theses that provide clarity to a Biblical understanding of the role of philosophy in education.
17 Luther, *Heidelberg Disputation*, 9.
18 Mattes, *Martin Luther's Theology of Beauty: A Reappraisal*, 161. With its emphasis on academic achievement, the contemporary Classical

education movement needs to be alert to the danger of this Platonic tendency to subordinate emotion to intellect. Luther had a more balanced view that integrated *intellectus* (understanding) and *affectus* (emotion) into education. While *intellectus* is essential for a proper understanding of theology, emotions also has a place in the life of the Christian.
19 Luther, Sermon on the Mount, *LW* 21:197-198.

Treatment Protocols

1 Erasmus, *De pueris instituendis* (1529), CWE 26, 339.
2 Douglas Murray, *The Madness of Crowds: Race, Gender, and Identity* (New York: Bloomsbury, 2019), 115-20.
3 I once developed an informal 20-question test that I administered to student teachers in Junior and Senior year of college. It covered matters that every elementary school teacher in America should know. The results were dismal: 43% couldn't identify July 4th as the date the Declaration of Independence is generally understood as being signed, 29% couldn't identify the contents of the 1st Amendment, 29% couldn't identify the president as the commander-in-chief of the armed forces, 58% couldn't identify America's enemies during WWII, and 72% couldn't identify the year that Japan attacked Pearl Harbor.
4 One of the criticisms of rote learning is that it ignores individual learning styles. This theory, which has come to dominate contemporary education, maintains that everyone learns differently and so teachers must be prepared to accommodate all the various learning styles of students. So ingrained is this doctrine that a whole industry is dedicated to producing curricular resources, assessments, and teacher training workshops to support this practice. However, according to several substantial studies, there is little evidence to support this theory and the research that supports it is often flawed or contradictory. One study concluded that "at present, there is no adequate evidence base to justify incorporating learning-style assessments into general educational practice." See Harold Pashler et al., "Learning Styles: Concepts and Evidence," *Journal of the Association for Psychological Science* 9, no. 3 (2008).
5 Aristotle had divided memory and recollection, and assigned different values to the two abilities. Quintilian said that the memory was the best indicator of a man's ability to learn. Augustine depicted the memory as the locus for learning, reasoning, imagination, and thought.
6 Luther, *Lectures on the Psalms* (1513-1515), *LW* 11:15.
7 Dome Karukoski, "Tolkien," (USA, May 10, 2019).
8 SC 3rd Commandment 352

9 LC 3rd Commandment 398
10 Dana Goldstein, "Why Kids Can't Write," *The New York Times* (New York City), August 06, 2017, Education Life.
11 Goldstein, "Why Kids Can't Write."
12 Another argument is that learning one of the sacred languages is of great value to STEM fields. For example, if students have mastered Latin, they have a much easier time learning computer programming. This is because programming is a language with its own vocabulary, syntax, and grammar. Learning a sacred language forces students to understand all languages–including programming–in a careful methodical way.
13 Luther *To the Councilmen of All Cities in Germany that they Establish and Maintain Christian Schools* (1524) LW 45:347-378.
14 This is not to say that Luther completely rejected the Pythagorian approach to music. He still valued the mathematical aspect of music and it continued to be part of Lutheran education. This mathematical aspect is evident in the works of Bach who weaves numerical messages into his compositions.
15 Luther, *Tischreden* (1538), WA Tr. 3, No. 3815.
16 Luther, *Tischreden*, WA Tr. 5, No. 6248.
17 Martin Luther, "Preface to George Rhau's Symphoniae Iucundae," in Michael Mark, *Source Readings in Music Education History* (New York: Macmillan, 1982), 74.
18 Every confession has its sacred music that is used to promote prayer and meditation: the Roman Catholic confession has the Gregorian chant, the Eastern Orthodox church has Byzantine chant, and the Reformed church has Psalm singing. The sacred music for the Evangelical Lutheran church is the chorale, a unique form of congregational song that is both doxological (giving praise to God) and catechetical. Where other hymns might focus on emotional appeals to the singer, the choral focuses on the proclamation of the Word of God with the understanding that God will work through the word to accomplished true faith. These hymns communicate a Lutheran piety and emphasize justification, cross and suffering, law and gospel, etc. It is widely recognized that the chorale became one of Lutheranism's great contributions to Western Christianity. For a suggested list of chorales to be taught in schools see Appendix 3
19 J. C. Vonderau, "Liederpensum für die Schule," *Evangelisch-Lutherisches Schulblatt* 26, no. 6 (June 1891).
20 Luther, *Tischreden*, WA Tr. 5, No. 3589.
21 In the nineteenth century, this title was taken away from theology and given to mathematics by the German mathematician, Johann Gauss. In spite of being raised in a Lutheran household, Gauss maintained that God was not revealed in Scripture. Science alone was capable of

transcending doctrinal theology to bring immortal truth to light. Gauss stated "Religion is not a question of literature, but of life. God's revelation is continuous, not contained in tablets of stone or sacred parchment. A book is inspired when it inspires" (G. Waldo Dunnington, Jeremy Gray, and Fritz-Egbert Dohse, *Carl Friedrich Gauss: Titan of Science* (Washington, DC: Mathematical Association of America, 2004), 301.

22 It is poorly named because the Enlightenment resulted in the very opposite of what it claimed. With its exaltation of reason above revelation, it lost the deeper understanding of life in creation that theology provided.

23 Barak Obama, "Remarks by the President at White House Science Fair," news release, 2015, https://obamawhitehouse.archives.gov/the-press-office/2015/03/23/remarks-president-white-house-science-fair.

24 Luther, *Lectures on Genesis* (1536) *LW* 1:46.

25 Peter Barker and Bernard R. Goldstein, "Theological Foundations of Kepler's Astronomy," *Osiris* 16, no. 1 (2001): 113, https://doi.org/10.1086/649340, https://www.journals.uchicago.edu/doi/abs/10.1086/649340.

26 Johannes Kepler, *Mysterium Cosmographicium* quoted in Barker and Goldstein, "Theological Foundations of Kepler's Astronomy," 82.

27 Richard Bulliet et al., eds., *The Earth and Its Peoples: A Global History* 5th ed., vol. II (Boston: Houghton Mifflin Company 2012), xiii-xiv.

28 Richard A. Carranza, June 03, 2020.

29 Luther, *To the Councilmen in All Cities in Germany* (1524), *LW* 45:376. This stood in contrast to humanists such as Erasmus for whom history was much more anthropocentric. By studying the lives of noble and virtuous people of the past, students would take on those qualities and would themselves become noble and virtuous.

30 Luther, *Vorrede D. M. L. auf die Historia Galeatii Capellae vom Herzog zu Mailand* (1538), WA 50:383–385, quoted in Franklin Verzelius Newton Painter, *Luther on Education* (St. Louis: Concordia Publishing House, 1928), 162.

31 Luther, *Treatise on Good Works* (1520), *LW* 44:95.

A Classical Liberal Arts Education: The Training of Christian Thinkers

1 At one school I visited, the teachers gathered once a week after school to spend time doing just that. They went from being teachers to students of the Scriptures and the Confessions of the church in order to discern how those things should shape their pedagogy and influence their curricular choices.

2 David Goodwin and David Sikkink, *Good Soil: A Comparative Study of ACCS Alumni Life Outcomes*, Association of Classical Christian Schools (January 27, 2020 2020), 6, https://www.classicaldifference.com/wp-content/uploads/2020/06/The-Classical-Difference-Good-Soil-7-outcomes-full-research-report-Draft-3-28-2020.pdf.
3 Often teachers have confided in me about how much of what they learned in college had to be discarded as soon as they got to the classroom. They often lament about how much of their time in school was wasted in reproducing lesson plans and forms that conformed to state standards. What they missed the most is the opportunity to learn more content.
4 William M. Smail, *Quintilian on Education: A Translation of Select Passage from the Institutio Oratoria* (New York, NY: Columbia Teacher College Press, 1938), 79.

Conclusion

1 Luther, *Sermon on the Estate of Marriage*, LW 44:12-13.

Appendices

1 This list was discovered by Scott Gercken. Scott Gercken, "The Missouri Synod's Drift Toward Rationalistic Pedagogy as Evidenced in Evangelisch-Lutherisches Schulblatt, 1889-1927" (Master of Arts in Religion Concordia University Chicago, 2020). The original is found in "Liederpensum für die Schule," *Evangelisch-Lutherisches Schulblatt* 26, no. 6 (June 1891), 176.
2 Cf. Carl Ferdinand Wilhelm Walther, *Kirchengesangbuch für Evangelisch-Lutherische Gemeinden ungeänerter Augsburgischer Konfession* (Saint Louis: Concordia Publishing House, n.d.).
3 English titles are drawn from Carl Ferdinand Wilhelm Walther, comp., *Walther's Hymnal: Church Hymnbook for Evangelical Lutheran Congregations of the Unaltered Augsburg Confession*, trans. and ed. by Matthew Carver (Saint Louis: Concordia Publishing House, 2012). Originally published as *Kirchen-gesangbuch für Evangelisch-Lutherische Gemeinden ungeänerter Augsburgischer Confession* (Saint Louis: Concordia Publishing House, 1892).
4 This may refer to a student catechism book like one of the many editions of the Johann Conrad Dietrich or Heinrich Christian Schwan's catechisms incorporating the text of *Luther's Small Catechism* as well as offering explanations of the catechism, proof-texts, psalms, and sometimes hymns.

Bibliography

"10 of the Best Growth Mindset Activites for Kids." no. July 09, 2020. https://wabisabilearning.com/blogs/mindfulness-wellbeing/growth-mindset-activities-kids.

"About Montessori Education." American Montessori Association, 2020, accessed July 01, 2020, https://amshq.org/About-Montessori.

"A Marxist Critique of John Dewey: The Limits of Progressive Education." Left Voice, 2017, accessed May 05, 2021, https://www.leftvoice.org/a-marxist-critique-of-john-dewey-the-limits-of-progressive-education/.

Aristotle. "Metaphysics." http://classics.mit.edu/Aristotle/metaphysics.13.xiii.html.

Augustine. "The Literal Meaning of Genesis, Book Iii." In *Ancient Christian Writers Series*, edited by John Hammond Taylor, Paulist Press, 1982.

———. *On Christian Doctrine*. Translated by James Shaw. Nicene and Post-Nicene Fathers. Edited by Philip Schaff. Vol. 2, Buffalo, NY: Christian Literature Publishing, 1887.

Barker, Peter, and Bernard R. Goldstein. "Theological Foundations of Kepler's Astronomy." *Osiris* 16, no. 1 (2001): 88-113. https://doi.org/10.1086/649340. https://www.journals.uchicago.edu/doi/abs/10.1086/649340.

Benedict, XVI. *Jesus of Nazareth*. San Francisco: Ignatius Press, 2011.

Bernard, of Clairvaux. "Sermons on the Songs of Songs, Sermon 1." In *The Works of Bernard of Clairvaux*, edited by Kilian Walsh Kalamazoo, MI: Kalamazoo Publications, 1981http://people.duke.edu/~dainotto/Texts/clairvaux.pdf.

"Classical Lutheran Education Defined." Institute for the Lutheran Liberal Arts, accessed January 05, 2020, http://illa.us.

Bowers, Chet. *Education for Eco-Justice and Community*. Athens, Georgia: University of Georgia Press, 2001.

Budzienski, Jaime. "Activities to Teach Toddlers with Vygotsky's Theory." (October 30, 2014 2014). Accessed July 09, 2020. https://howtoadult.com/activities-teach-toddlers-vygotskys-theory-16606.html.

Bulliet, Richard, Pamela Kyle Crossley, Daniel Headrick, Steven Hirsch, Lyman Johnson, and David Northrup, eds. *The Earth and Its Peoples: A Global History* 5th ed Vol. II. Boston: Houghton Mifflin Company 2012.

Burfeind, Peter. *Gnostic America*. Pax Domini Press, 2014.

Callaway, Webster. *Jean Piaget: A Most Outrageous Deception*. New York: Nova Science Publishers, 2001.

Carnes, Mark C., and Gary Kates. *Rousseau, Burke and Revolution in France, 1791*. "Reacting to the Past" Series. New York: Pearson Longman, 2005.

Chapman, Michael. *Constructive Evolution : Origins and Development of Piaget's Thought*. Cambridge England ; New York: Cambridge University Press, 1988. http://www.loc.gov/catdir/description/cam023/87021816.html.

Dewey, John. *The Human Nature and Conduct: An Introduction to Social Psychology*. New York: Henry Holt, 1922.

———. "Impressions of Soviet Russia." In *John Dewey: The Later Works*, edited by Jo Ann Boydston.

———. "My Pedagogic Creed." *School Journal* 54, no. January (1897): 77-80. 1897.

Dunnington, G. Waldo, Jeremy Gray, and Fritz-Egbert Dohse. *Carl Friedrich Gauss : Titan of Science*. Washington, DC: Mathematical Association of America, 2004.

Egan, Kieran. *Getting It Wrong from the Beginning : Our Progressivist Inheritance from Herbert Spencer, John Dewey, and Jean Piaget*. New Haven: Yale University Press, 2002.

Feinberg, Walter. "Religious Education in Liberal Democratic Societies: The Question of Accountability and Autonomy." In *Education and Citizenship in Liberal-Democratic Societies: Teaching for Cosmopolitan Values and Collective Identities*, edited by Kevin McDonough and Walter Feinberg. Oxford: Oxford University Press, 2003.

Frankforter. *The Theologia Germanica of Martin Luther*. The Classics of Western Spirituality. Edited by Bengt R. Hoffman. New York: Paulist Press, 1980.

Fraser, Jennifer, and Anton Yasnitsky. "Deconstructing Vygotsky's Victimization Narrative: A Re-Examination of the 'Stalinist Suppression' of Vygotskian Theory." *History of the Human Sciences* 28, no. 2 (2015): 128-53. https://doi.org/10.1177/0952695114560200.

Froebel, Friedrich. "Education of Man." Translated by Irene M. Lilley. In *Friedrich Froebel: A Selection from His Writings*. London: Cambridge University Press, 1967.

Gentry, Austin, "Steve Jobs & Religion," August 19, 2016, https://www.austingentry.com/steve-jobs-religion/.

Gercken, Scott. "The Missouri Synod's Drift toward Rationalistic Pedagogy as Evidenced in Evangelisch-Lutherisches Schulblatt, 1889-1927." Master of Arts in Religion, Concordia University Chicago, 2020.

Goldstein, Dana. "Why Kids Can't Write." *The New York Times* (New York City), August 06, 2017, Education Life, 8.

Goodwin, David, and David Sikkink. *Good Soil: A Comparative Study of Accs Alumni Life Outcomes*. Association of Classical Christian Schools (January 27, 2020 2020). https://www.classicaldifference.com/wp-content/uploads/2020/06/The-Classical-Difference-Good-Soil-7-outcomes-full-research-report-Draft-3-28-2020.pdf.

Hill, Dave. "Marxist Education against Capitalism in Neoliberal/Neoconservative Times." Chap. 13 In *Marxism and Education*, edited by L. Rasinski, D. Hill and K. Skordoulis, 160-82. New York: Routledge, 2018.

Hull, John M. "Atheism and the Future of Religious Eduction." In *Crossing the Boundaries: Essays in Biblical Interpretation in Honour of Michael D. Goulder*, edited by Stanley Porter, Paul Joyce and David Orton, 357-75. Leiden: Brill, 1994.

"Humanist Manifesto." 1933, accessed November 24, 2019, https://americanhumanist.org/what-is-humanism/manifesto1/.

"What Is Classical Education?", accessed August 21, 2019, https://www.circeinstitute.org/resources/what-classical-education.

Karukoski, Dome. "Tolkien." 112. USA, May 10, 2019 2019.

Levinson, Meira. *The Demands of Liberal Education*. New York: Oxford University Press, 1999.

Lewy, Guenter. *If God Is Dead Everything Is Permitted*. New Brunswick, New Jersey: Transaction Publishers, 2008.

Liben, Lynn S. *Piaget and the Foundations of Knowledge*. The Jean Piaget Symposium Series. Hillsdale, N.J.: L. Erlbaum Associates, 1983.

Luther, Martin. *Heidelberg Disputation*. Holt, MO: Higher Things Inc, 2018.

———. *What Luther Says: An Anthology*. Edited by Ewald M. Plass. Vol. I, St. Louis, MO: Concordia Publishing, 1959.

Mark, Michael. *Source Readings in Music Education History*. New York: Macmillian, 1982.

Mattis, Mark. *Martin Luther's Theology of Beauty: A Reappraisal*. Grand Rapids, MI: Baker Academic, 2017.

Michigan K-12 Standards: English Language Arts.

Millennials and Their Retention since Confirmation. Lutheran Church-Missouri Synod (2017). http://www.youthesource.com/wp-content/uploads/2018/04/Millennials-Congregation-Confirmation-Survey-Report.pdf.

Mitchell, Mike, and Walt Dohrn. "Trolls." 2016.

Montessori, Maria. *The Aborsbant Mind*. Oxford, England: Clio Press, 1988.

———. *Education and Peace*. Translated by Helen Lane. Chicago: Henry Regnery, 1972.

———. *The Secret of Childhood*. Translated by Joseph Costelloe. Indiana: Fides Publishers, 1966.

———. *To Educate the Human Potential*. Madras, India: Kalakshetra Publications, 1955.

Murray, Douglas. *The Madness of Crowds: Race, Gender, and Identity*. New York: Bloomsbury, 2019.

O'Donnell, Erin. "The Risks of Homeschooling." *Harvard Magazine*, no. May-June 2020. (2020). Accessed July 06, 2020. https://www.harvardmagazine.com/2020/05/right-now-risks-homeschooling.
Obama, Barak. "Remarks by the President at White House Science Fair." news release, 2015, https://obamawhitehouse.archives.gov/the-press-office/2015/03/23/remarks-president-white-house-science-fair.
Pagels, Elaine. *Adam, Eve, and the Serpent*. New York: Random House, 1988.
Painter, Franklin Verzelius Newton. *Luther on Education*. St. Louis: Concordia Publishing House, 1928.
Pashler, Harold, Mark McDaniel, Doug Rohrer, and Robert Bjork. "Learning Styles: Concepts and Evidence." *Journal of the Association for Psychological Science* 9, no. 3 (2008): 105-19.
Pestalozzi, Johann Heinrich. *The Education of Man*. Translated by William H. Kilpatrick. New York: Greenwood Press, 1969.
Pinzger, Gustav. *Valentin Friedland Trotzendorf Dargestellt. Mit Trotzendorfs Bildniss Und Facsimile Seiner Handschrift*. Hirschberg, 1825.
Plato. *The Republic*. Translated by Benjamin Jowett. Mineola, New York: Dover, 2000.
Rousseau, Jean Jacques. *The Social Contract*. Translated by Charles Frankel. New York: Hafner Publishing, 1947.
———. *Social Contract and Discourses*. New York: Dutton, 1913. https://www.bartleby.com/168/.
Sasse, Hermann. *Scripture and the Church: Select Essays of Hermann Sasse*. Edited by Ronald R. Feuerhahn and Jeffery J. Kloha. St. Louis, MO: Concordia Seminary, 1995.
Scaer, David P. "Doctrine of Election: A Lutheran Note." Chap. 9 In *Perspectives on Evangelical Theology*, edited by Stanley N. Gundy. Indiana: Baker, 1979.
Schaff, Philip, and Henry Wace. *A Select Library of Nicene and Post-Nicene Fathers of the Christian Church. Second Series*. 14 vols. Vol. II, New York: The Christian literature company; etc., 1890.
Sève, Lucien. "Where Is Marx in the Work and Thought of Vygotsky." 7e Seminaire International Vygotski, 20-22 juin 2018 2018.
Shiraev, Eric. *A History of Psychology*. Washington: Sage, 2011.
Smail, William M. *Quintilian on Education: A Translation of Select Passage from the Institutio Oratoria*. New York, NY: Columbia Teacher College Press, 1938.
Smith, Katy. "New Roles, New Relationships." *Educational Leadership* 51, no. 2 (1993).
Spencer, Herbert. *Essays on Education and Kindred Subjects*. Everyman's Library, Ed by Ernest Rhys Essays. London: J. M. Dent & Sons, 1916.
Spencer, Herbert. "The Importance of Science." In *Readings in the History of Education*, edited by Ellwood P. Cubberly, 659-61. Chicago: Houghton Mifflin, 1920.
Toulmin, Stephen. "The Mozart of Psychology." Book Review, *New York Times*, September 28, 1979.

Vidal, Fernado. *Piaget before Piaget*. Cambridge, Mass: Harvard University Press, 1994.

Vonderau, J. C. "Liederpensum Für Die Schule." *Evangelisch-Lutherisches Schulblatt* 26, no. 6 (June 1891 1891): 171-77.

Vygotsky, L. S. "Educational Psychology." Florida: St. Lucie Press, 1926https://www.marxists.org/archive/vygotsky/works/1926/educational-psychology/index.htm.

———. "The Socialist Alteration of Man." In *Vygotsky Reader,* edited by Rene van der Veer and Jaan ValsinerBlackwell, 1930https://www.marxists.org/archive/vygotsky/works/1930/socialism.htm.

Vygotsky, L. S., R. W. Rieber, David Kent Robinson, and Jerome S. Bruner. *The Essential Vygotsky*. New York: Kluwer Academic/Plenum Publishers, 2004.

Warde, W. F. "The Fate of Dewey's Theories." *International Socialist Review* 21, no. 2 (1960): 54-57, 61. https://www.marxists.org/archive/novack/works/1960/x04.htm.

Weor, Samael Aun. *Fundamentals of Gnostic Education*. Brooklyn NY: Glorian, 2013.

Scripture index

Genesis
  1:28, 56
  6-9, 2
Exodus
  33:23, 84
Psalms
  51:3, 48
  51:5, 49
Matthew
  8, 25
John
  17:3, 43
  18:37, 76
Romans
  7:12, 84
  7:18-19, 81
  8:29, 77
  13:1, 51

1 Corinthians
  1:25, 85
  1:27-28, 85
Ephesians
  3:8-10, 78–79
  4:6, 65, 99
  4:29, 45
  5:27, 53
Philippians
  4:8, 17
  4:8-9, 81
Colossians
  2:8, 111
Titus
  2:1, 57
1 Peter
  2:9, 49
  4:10, 133n7

Subject index

activity-based learning, 19
aeons, 24, 35
American democracy, 33
American educationalists
    German educationalists and, 129n1
    Piaget's influence on, 22
    Vygotsky and, 17–19
ancient Greek schools
    on beauty, 73–74
    on goodness, 72
    Platonic ideals, 71, 79–82
    On senses, 130n4
    on Truth, 76
    on unity, 78
Anglican Communion, 134n12
Apostles' Creed, 10, 11, 37, 47, 90
Athanasian Creed, 78
atheism, 10, 131n14
atheology, 8
Augsburg Confession, 121
authorities instituted by God
    about, 51–52
    estate of the church, 52–54
    estate of the family, 55–57
    estate of the government, 54–55
    rejection of, 42
authority
    of church, 108, 134n13
    of collective, 12, 16

critical thinking and, 117
external authority, 134n13
goodness and, 133n1
of governments, 54
intellectual authority, 11
internal authority, 134n13
liberal education and, 33–34
rejection of, 51–52, 65
of self, 65, 134n13
of teachers, 116
under Marxism, 12, 16–17
autonomy, 32–33, 34, 49, 128n8

baptism, 49–50, 61, 79, 85
beauty
    ancient Greek schools on, 73–74, 79–80
    in Christian education, 71
    Progressive Education and, 75
    Rousseau on, 31, 32
    as subjective, 75
    theologians on, 74–75
    Vygotsky on, 15
    wisdom and, 47
belief systems
    educational models and, 3
    Levinson on, 32–33
    Progressive Education and, 9–10
Book of Concord, 134n12

SUBJECT INDEX

bourgeois morality, 15
Boy Scout Movement, 124n12
Branch (fictional character), 36
Byzantine chant, 136n18

Camino Santiago, 134n13
capitalism
   neo-Marxists on, 18
   Secular Humanism and, 8, 125n25
   Vygotsky on, 16
Cartesian dualism, 23
catechesis
   Bernard on, 61
   in Christian schools, 132n25
   education and, 61–62
   indoctrination and, 32
   Luther on, 60
   rejection of, 57–62
character development, 117
child development theory, 22, 24
chorale, 120–21, 136n18
Christian colleges of education, xii, xiii, 59
Christian educational heritage, recovery of, xiii, 112–113
Christian educators
   contemporary educational theory and, 28
   educational theories and, xiv
   on independent learning, 129n15
   Piaget's views and, 26–27
   response of, 43
   training of, 105–110
Christian morality, 15–16
Christian schools
   curriculum of, 90–103
   Feinberg on, 33
   learning about sin in, 50–51
   Levinson on, 32, 33
Christianity
   Dewey on, 10–11
   Piaget on, 24
church
   authority of, 108, 134n13

education and, 5
   as ruling elite, 15
civic righteousness, 49
classical Christian education
   comparison of, 115–117
   Progressive education and, 12–13
classical education
   Gnostic education on, 39–40
   Montessori on curriculum for, 21
   Piaget on, 25
   rejection of, 15, 16
Classical education movement, 135n18
classical liberal arts education, 30, 79, 80–81, 105–110
cognitive development theory of Piaget, 7, 22, 25, 26–27
Cold War, 13
collective morality, 16–17
colleges of education, xii
   Gnosticism and, 38–39, 42
   government funding, xiii
   marketing, xiii
   Piaget's influence on, 22, 25
   standard canon of educational thinkers and, 1, 7
Communism
   Dewey and, 11–12
   Vygotsky and, 14
Communist Revolution, 11, 14
contemporary educational theory
   Christian educators and, 28
   Rousseau and, 31–32
content and methods, 87–90, 117
corporal punishment, 131n13
Creative Evolution (Bergson), 23
creeds
   Apostles' Creed, 10, 11, 37, 47, 90
   Athanasian Creed, 78
   My Pedagogic Creed (Dewey), 10, 12
   in secular education, 37–38
critical thinking, 18, 29, 30–34, 117
Crusades, 131n14
curriculum
   comparison of, 117

SUBJECT INDEX

development of, 9
hidden curriculums, 18
Montessori on, 21
underlying agendas in choice of, xii
curriculum of the Christian school
  history, 101–103
  language, 91–95
  Montessori on, 21
  music, 95–98
  sciences, 98–101
  teachers and, 90–91
  unity and, 77

Darth Vader (fictional character), 36
dialectic materialism theory, 15
discipline
  corporal punishment, 131n13
  external discipline, 39
  Law and, 50
  of learning, 36
  spiritual discipline, 66
  teachers and, 50, 131n13
divine design, 133n1
divinity, 20–21
dodgeball, 48, 131n11
dualism, 23

early childhood education, 7, 19
Eastern Orthodox Church, 136n18
education
  Christian approach to, xiii
  Enlightenment and, 5–8
  Froebel on, 6
  Pestalozzi on, 5
  Spencer on, 6–7
  subjects in, 78
  theology and, xiii, 1
  until 19th century, 4–5
educational philosophy, Gnosticism and, 34–40
educational theories. *See also* effects of educational theories
  basis of, xii
  belief systems and, 7–8
  effects of experimental educational approaches, 131n12
  of Christian educational thinkers, xiii
  Gnosticism and, 35
  Rousseau and, 31–32
  theology and, xii, xiii
educationalists
  in 20th century, 4, 129n1
  German educationalists, 129n1
  goodness and, 133n1
  personal beliefs of, 1–3
  theological bias of, 3
effects of educational theories
  harm to individuals, 63–65
  harm to society, 67–68
  harm to the church, 65–66
elitism
  Dewey on, 10
  neo-Marxists and, 18, 54
  Progressive Education and, 13
  Vygotsky on, 15
emancipatory pedagogy, 18
Émile (Rousseau), 31
emotions, 79–80
empirical research, 43–44
empowerment, 48, 57
Enlightenment
  critical thinking and, 30
  Dewey on, 10
  educationalists and, 5–8
  French Revolution and, 128n7
  goals of, 80
  as misnamed, 127–128n1, 137n22
  Montessori and, 20
  Original Sin and, 48, 49
  Pestalozzi and, 42
  theology and, 99
environmental justice, 18
ethics
  goodness as, 72, 99
  Scientism and, 130n3
  of Secular Humanism, 13
  theology and, 71

Evangelical Lutheran Church
  on Platonic ideals, 81–82
  Reformers on theology of, 5
  sacred music of, 136n18
  on Scripture, xiii
evolution
  Bergson on, 23
  Dewey and, 8, 10
  education and, 6–7
  Montessori and, 20–21
  Piaget and, 23, 26
  Übermensch (superman), 125–126n32
exposure, 126n41

faith
  in classical theology, 59
  faith development, 59
  Fowler on, 27
Faith Development Theory, 27
fides qua creditur, 59–60
fides quae creditur, 59–60
freedom
  liberal education on, 33
  Weor on, 39
French Revolution, 128n7
The Fundamentals of Gnostic Education
  (Weor), 38–39

games, xii, 48, 131n11
genetic epistemology, 22
German educationalists, 129n1
gnosis, 35
Gnostic America (Burfeind), 37
Gnosticism
  cognitive development theory, 26–27
  defined, 21
  education and, 34–40
  Fowler and, 27
  German influence on, 129n1
  Leibniz and, 24
  liberal education and, 42
  Montessori and, 7, 19–22
  myth and, 128n12

Piaget and, 7, 22–27
popular culture and, 35–36, 40
Theory of Faith Development, 27
Truth and, 129n16
Gnostics, 19–27, 129n12
God
  beauty and, 74–75
  knowledge of, 49
  Leibniz on, 24
  Luther on, 45–46
  Piaget on, 23–25
  rejection of belief in, 10, 15
  Weor on, 39
  wrath of, xiii
gods
  in Gnosticism, 24, 25, 35
  Plato on, 130n2
  of Roman mythology, 47, 76
goodness
  ancient Greek schools on, 72, 79–80
  in Christian education, 71
  measuring of, 133n1
  Rousseau on, 30–31, 32
  Vygotsky on, 15
  wisdom and, 47
Gospel
  Law and, 132n20
  lens of, xiii–xiv
government funding
  of college programs, xiii
  for research, 132n15
government-run education
  Christian schools and, 54, 111–112
  liberal education and, 32–33, 34
grace, 133n8
grading, 132n20
Gregorian chant, 136n18
Growth Mindset, 2

Harry Potter (film series), 35
Heidelberg Catechism, 134n12
Heidelberg Disputation, 83, 84
heresies, 21, 34–35
heroes, 130n2

SUBJECT INDEX

hidden curriculums, 18
homeschooling, 33
hope, 126n32
human nature, 21
Humanists, 137n28
The Humanist Manifesto (1933), 8, 10
hymns
    for Augsburg Confession, 121
    communal singing of, 96–98
    Learn-by-Heart Schdule of Hymns, 118–120
    for Six Chief Parts of Luther's Small Catechism, 120

ignorance, 127–128n1
independent learning, 129n15
individualism
    Dewey on, 10–11
    Secular Humanists on, 125n25
indoctrination, 32, 34, 42, 57–58
instruction, 116
intelligent design, 133n1

Janissaries, 111
Jesus Christ
    Gospel and, xiii
    science as domain of, 100
    Truth and, 76–77

Kindergarten, 6, 18, 129n1
knowledge
    authority and, 116
    curriculum and, 117
    divisions of, 98, 133n7
    in Gnosticism, 35
    Piaget on, 22, 25
    religion and, 130n3
    science and, 130n3
    Secular Humanists on, 124n18
    senses and, 130n4
    theology and, 1
    Weor on, 39
    ZPD theory and, 16

languages, 126n41
Latin
    importance of learning, 136n12
    rejection of, 16
Law
    autonomy at expense of, 49
    Gospel and, 132n20
    as guidance, 50
    indoctrination and, 58–59
    lens of, xiii–xiv
    standards and, 84
Learn-by-Heart Schedule of Hymns, 118–120
learning styles, 135n4
Leninism, 17–18
liberal education
    autonomy and, 32–33, 34, 128n8
    comparison of, 115–117
    comparison to classical Christian education, 115–117
    critical thinking, 29–34
    German influence on, 129n1
    Gnostic education and, 42
    Gnosticism, 34–40
    Rousseau and, 31–32
liberatory pedagogy, 18
Liederpensum, 97, 118
Lucifer, 35
Luke Skywalker (fictional character), 36

The Madness of Crowds (Murray), 88
marriage, rejection of, 128n12
Marxism
    German influence on Marxist Education, 129n1
    on governments, 54
    on hope, 126n32
    introduction of, 126n37
    liberal education and, 42
    neo-Marxists, 18, 88, 92–93, 95
    psychology of, 14–15
    religion and, 126n32
    Vygotsky and, 7, 13–19

Marxists, 13–19
  critique by, 125n25
  on Dewey's educational ideas, 125n29
  educationalists, 14
  Vygotskian Theory, 125n27
materialism, 125n25
mathematics
  music and, 136n14
  sciences and, 98
  truth and, 136n21
The Matrix (film series), 35, 36
Mazda Miata analogy, 133n2
memory, 135n5
"Metaphysics" (Aristotle), 133n5
Mind in Society (Vygotsky), 18
mission of the church, xiv
Molly Brawn (Hungerford), 74
Monad, 24, 25, 35
Montessori education, 7, 19
morality
  as elitist construct, 18
  Vygotsky on, 15–16
Morpheus (fictional character), 36
Mr. Spock (fictional character), 80
music, 95–98, 136n14. See also hymns; sacred music
My Pedagogic Creed (Dewey), 10, 12
mysticism, 24, 26, 129n1
myth, 128n12

natural impulses, 31, 128n7
natural interest, 126n41
natural sciences, 2, 128n2, 130n4
nature of child, 115
nature of truth, 116. See also truth
Neo (fictional character), 36
neo-Marxists, 18, 88, 92–93, 95
Neo-Platonists, 82
95 Theses, 57
No Citizen Left Behind, 128n9

objectives, 116
"On Christian Doctrine" (Augustine), 5

"On the Moral Effects of the Arts and Sciences" (Rousseau), 30
"On the Six Cornered Snowflake" (Kepler), 47
order
  as oppressive, 40
  underlying the universe, 131n9
Original Sin
  Anglican Communion on, 134n12
  Gnostics and, 129n12
  Montessori on, 20, 22
  Piaget on, 24
  rejection of, 42, 48–51
The Origin of Species (Darwin), 6
outcomes, 117

parents
  Bartholet on, 33–34
  estate of family, 55–57
  Levinson on, 32–33
  response of, 43
  Weor on, 39
pastors
  contemporary educational theory and, 28
  Faith Development Theory and, 27
  response of, 43
persecutions in 20th century, 131–132n14
personal beliefs, xii, 1–3
philosophy
  Christian educational philosophy and, xiii
  classical categories of, 128n2
  Gnosticism and, 35
  poetry and, 130n6
  role in education, 134n16
  senses and, 130n4
Pietism, 41–43, 131n13
pilgrimages, 134n13
Pink Floyd, 39–40
Platonic ideals, 81–83
pleroma, 35
poetry, 130n6

SUBJECT INDEX

popular culture
　gnostic doctrine and, 35
　vulgarity in, 3
positive affirmation, 48
Preface to the Large Catechism, 60, 62
Progressive Education
　beauty and, 75
　Classical Christian education and, 12–13
　Communism and, 11–12
　comparison of, 115–117
　defined, 9
　Dewey and, 9
　The Humanist Manifesto (1933) and, 9
　My Pedagogic Creed (Dewey), 10, 12
　on teaching process, 9
Psalm singing, 136n18
psychology
　Christian educational philosophy and, xiii
　education and, 6–7
　faith and, 27
　of Marxism, 14–15
　Piaget and, 26
　research in, 2
　Sabatier on, 23
　theology and, 6–7
　Vygotskian Theory, 7, 13, 125n27
Pythagorian approach to music, 136n14

Quadrivium, 98

radical feminism, 128–129n12
Rationalism, 41–43
redemption, 20
Reformation, 94, 130n6
Reformed church
　Piaget and, 23
　sacred music of, 136n18
Reformers, on education, 5
Relativism, 117
religion. *See also* Christianity
　Dewey on, 10–11, 12–13
　knowledge and, 130n3
　Marxism and, 126n32
　Piaget on, 23
　Rousseau on, 31
religion class
　as catechesis, 132n25
　grading, 132n20
　theology restricted t, 46
　theology restricted to, 112
Renaissance, 30
The Republic (Plato), 43, 80, 130n2
research
　assumptions about, 1–3
　empirical research, 43–44
Revelation
　rejection of Truth through, 7, 43–48
　Scripture as, xiii
Roman Catholic Church
　Montessori's affiliation with, 19–20, 127n42
　sacred music of, 136n18
rote learning
　criticisms of, 116, 135n4
　encouragement of, 116

sacred music
　Hymn Assignments per Classroom, 120
　importance of, 136n18
　Learn-by-Heart Schedule of Hymns, 118–119
　matching hymns, 120–121
salvation
　Gnosticism on, 21
　liberal education on, 33
　Montessori on, 20
　Scientism and, 130n3
science
　Bergson on, 23
　Dewey on, 11
　faith and, 27
　knowledge and, 130n3
　Montessori method, 19
　Piaget on, 23, 25–26
　Secular Humanists on, 124n18

Space Race and, 13
  truth and, 136–137n21
sciences, classical categories of, 128n2
Scientism, 43–44, 130n3
Scripture
  Christian educational philosophy and, xiii–xiv
  education and, xiii
  Luther on, 44–45
  Montessori on, 20
  Piaget on, 26
  Pietism and, 41
  Rationalism and, 41
  revelation of truth and wisdom in, 44
  Sabatier on, 23
  theology and, xiii
  truth and, 127–128n1, 136–137n21
secular education
  Christian educators and, 27
  colleges of education, xii
  creeds in, 37–38
  faith development, 59
Secular Humanism
  Dewey and, 8–13
  theological views of Dewey, 7
Secular Humanists, 124n15
  atrocities and, 131n14
  on capitalism, 125n25
  on individualism, 125n25
  on knowledge, 124n18
  on materialism, 125n25
  on science, 124n18
self-actualization, 117
self-esteem, 48, 117
self-rule, 32–33
senses, 130n4
Sermon on Sending Children to School (Luther), 54–55
sin. *See also* Original Sin
  baptism and, 49–50
  estate of the government and, 54
  forgiveness of, 49–50, 53
  in Gnosticism, 35
  learning about, 50

  nature of child and, 115
  Scripture on, xiii
Small Catechism, 56, 120
social constructivism, 7, 17
The Social Contract (Rousseau), 30–31
social engineering, 33
social evolution
  education and, 6–7
  The Humanist Manifesto (1933) and, 9
  Vygotsky and, 14
social justice, 18
social science, 130n4
socialism, 17
sociology
  Christian educational philosophy and, xiii
  research in, 2
Sophia (mythic figure), 35
souls, 127n43
Soviet Union, 11–12
Space Race, 13
Spanish Inquisition, 131n14
Stages of Faith (Fowler), 27, 132n21
standards
  about, 71, 85–86
  Beauty, 71, 73–75
  Goodness, 71, 72–73
  Truth, 71, 76–77
  Unity, 71, 77–79
  using in wrong way, 79–85
Star Wars (film series), 35–36
Start Trek (TV series), 80
state licensure, xii
STEM fields, 136n12
structure
  beauty and, 74–75
  in creation, 47
  as oppressive, 40
student teaching, xii, 135n3
subjects
  in classical Christian education, 117
  in contemporary education, 78, 117

SUBJECT INDEX

teachers
  comparison of, 116
  contemporary educational theory and, 28
  curriculum development by, 9
  as disciplinarian, 131n13
  Faith Development Theory and, 27, 59
  Montessori method, 19
  Montessori on, 21
  Piaget on, 22, 26, 56
  primary role of, xii
  role in classical Christian education, 116
  role in liberal education, 116
  role in Progressive Education, 13
  state licensure of, xii
  training of, 19, 59, 105–110, 137n2, 138n4
  Waters on, 40
  Weor on, 39
  ZPD theory and, 17
teaching methods, xii, 87–90, 117
Theologia Germanica, ix, 83
theologians
  on beauty, 74–75
  on education, xiii
  Piaget's views and, 26–27
theological views
  of Dewey, 7, 10
  effects on educational theories, 7–8, 42–43
  of Montessori, 7, 19–22, 21
  of Piaget, 7, 22–25
  theological bias of educationalists, 3
  of Vygotsky, 7, 14–15
theology
  in ancient Greek schools, 71
  as divine philosophy, 128n2
  education and, xiii, 1, 46
  education theories and, xii
  knowledge and, 1
  psychology and, 6–7
  rejection of, 16
  sciences and, 98–101
  truth and, 136–137n21
Theory of Faith Development, 27
"Thirty-Nine Articles of Religion," 134n12
Thought and Language (Vygotsky), 17–18
To the Councilmen in All Cities in Germany (Luther), 102
Tolkien (film), 91
treatment protocols
  content and methods, 87–90
  curriculum of the Christian school, 90–103
Trinity, xiii, 78
Trivium, 98
Trolls (animated film), 36
Truth
  ancient Greek schools on, 76, 79–80
  Benedict XVI on, 77
  in Christian education, 71
  Enlightenment and, 127–128n1
  Fowler on, 27
  Gnosticism and, 129n16
  Levinson on, 32–33
  Luther on, 44–45
  nature of, 116
  Piaget on, 25
  in popular culture, 36
  rejection of Truth through Revelation, 7, 42, 43–48
  Rousseau on, 30–31, 32
  scientism on, 43–44
  in Scripture, 44–45
  Vygotsky on, 15
  wisdom and, 47

Übermensch (superman), 125–126n32
unity, 71, 77–79

values
  Levinson on, 32–33
  Weor on, 39

Vygotskian Theory, 7, 13, 15, 125n27.
    See also Zones of Proximal Development (ZPD)

Waldorf schools, 124n12
The Wall (song) (Pink Floyd), 39–40
whole child approach, 117
wisdom
    discovery of, 47
    as objective, 116

Piaget on, 25
in popular culture, 36
Rousseau on, 31
in Scripture, 44
wrath of God, xiii

Yaltabaoth (mythic figure), 35

Zones of Proximal Development (ZPD), 16–17. *See also* Vygotskian Theory

Made in the USA
Monee, IL
24 September 2024